Thor's OS Xodus

Thor's OS Xodus

Why And How I Left Windows For OS X

Timothy "Thor" Mullen
With
Katherine Ridgway

Russ Rogers, Technical Editor

ELSEVIER

AMSTERDAM • BOSTON • HEIDELBERG • LONDON
NEW YORK • OXFORD • PARIS • SAN DIEGO
SAN FRANCISCO • SINGAPORE • SYDNEY • TOKYO
Syngress is an imprint of Elsevier

SYNGRESS,

Acquiring Editor: Chris Katsaropoulos
Editorial Project Manager: Anna Valutkevich
Project Manager: Punithavathy Govindaradjane
Designer: Matthew Limbert

Syngress is an imprint of Elsevier
225 Wyman Street, Waltham, MA 02451, USA

ISBN: 978-0-12-410463-1

British Library Cataloguing-in-Publication Data
A catalogue record for this book is available from the British Library.

Library of Congress Cataloging-in-Publication Data
A catalog record for this book is available from the Library of Congress.

For Information on all Syngress publications
visit our website at http://store.elsevier.com/Syngress

www.elsevier.com • www.bookaid.org

Dedication

This book is for Steve Moffat, my dear friend who we lost last year. I lost both my mother and step father within months of each other last year as well, but they're cool and will understand why I'm dedicating the book to Steve. I've poked fun at Steve and my other friend Greg many times in my last few books and this book is no different. I thought it appropriate to keep all the references to Steve intact as he was a wonderful friend and a good man. Steve, I love you man. I'll see you on the other side. And I want the $50 you owe me.

Shout-outs to the little PNut even though he's been plucked away and I'll probably never get to see him again. Rock on, P. But I still want that $50 you owe me.

Finally, I'd like to thank Katie Ridgway who became one of my best friends this year and who not only helped me with edits in the book but also provided some much-needed motivation to get things done. She's too smart and too pretty, but just the right amount of Goof. Fly on Little Wing. I'll pay you that $100 I owe you as soon as a couple of slackers I know pay me back.

Contents

CHAPTER 1 OS X, Privacy, and Online Safety 1

Section One: Logical Privacy and Security 1

The Emperor Has No Clothes. And Neither Do You! 5

Section Two: Technical Privacy and Security –

Limiting Access to Sites 8

Firefox "Profiles" 15

Alternate Search Engines 20

TOR Proxy 21

Advanced Configuration Example: Low Level Firefox

Profile and Configuration Editing 26

Advanced+ Configuration Example: Shared Tor Proxy in

Virtual DMZ Environment 31

CHAPTER 2 OS Xodus – Media 55

Step #1: Basic Media Sharing via iTunes 58

Step #2: Advanced Media Control 67

AirPlay 67

CHAPTER 3 The Interface 75

Multiple Monitors and Customization 75

Finder and Navigation 78

Quick Look 85

Tags 86

Tagging With Spotlight 88

Apple Defaults and Script Editor 93

Encrypted Disk Images 99

Intelligent, Multi-Choice Dialog Boxes 108

Intelligent Shared File System Updates 110

Intelligent File Copy 116

CHAPTER 4 OS Xodus: Remote Access 123

VNC 124

Apple Remote Desktop 127

iCloud's Back to My Mac 137

SSH Supplement – Advanced Section 148

CHAPTER 5   OS X Server... 159

Medium Level Tech.. 161

Here's what we'll do in the medium section............................... *161*

Advanced Level Tech 180

Here's what we'll do in the advanced section............................ *180*

Starting and Configuration of Mail... *181*

Postfix Mail Services *192*

INDEX.. 207

OS X, Privacy, and Online Safety
Technical Classes: Basic, Standard, Advanced, and Advanced+

SECTION ONE: LOGICAL PRIVACY AND SECURITY

I feel confident in saying privacy and safety will be the most important concerns you will have (or should have) in your online life. And if they aren't now, they will be as time passes on.

For purposes of this chapter, I'm defining "privacy" as the level of control one has over their own personal information as well as the level of control one has as it regards personal information *other people own*. "Online safety" is primarily the ability to prevent unauthorized code from being executed on a system, including the specific controls one has in place to prevent code execution. That extends to preventing information disclosure, unauthorized access to files, application permissions, and so forth.

In actuality, privacy and security are fibers of the same cloth. They can be distinct concepts on their own, or they can be intimately entwined with each other. As such, I'm not going to try to classify every risk we discuss as one or the other; you are smart enough to switch to OS X, so you are smart enough to figure that part out.

I'll be discussing techniques and procedures specific to OS X, those distantly related to OS X, and in a case or two, processes that stand on their own irrespective of the OS one may be using. It's all part of the Big Privacy Picture, and though it may deviate a bit, I consider it required reading material. I'm calling this "logical security" as it does not apply to any particular technical security control, but rather behavioral changes you may wish to make in order to protect your data. So let's get started.

Internet advertising is the bane of the internet, and the core driver of the deep, vast violation of your personal privacy. These days, ad "impressions" don't mean anything. An ad "impression" is where there is some ad on a page somewhere, where the host assumes you looked at it; then bills the advertiser for aggregated impressions. Today, the "conversion" is the golden egg. You are the goose who wasn't aware you laid it. The conversion is where you

CONTENTS

Section One: Logical Privacy and Security 1
The Emperor Has No Clothes. And Neither Do You! 5

Section Two: Technical Privacy and Security – Limiting Access to Sites 8
Firefox "Profiles" 15
Alternate Search Engines 20
TOR Proxy 21
Advanced Configuration Example: Low Level Firefox Profile and Configuration Editing 26
Advanced+ Configuration Example: Shared Tor Proxy in Virtual DMZ Environment 31

are on a site, see an ad, click it, and end up buying whatever the advertiser is selling. Those are big money. It's such big money that the advertising hosts (those who produce the ads for the host site) have technology where they collect and analyze your personal information and browsing history to not only provide an ad, but to provide an ad specially selected for you, based on your browsing patterns and purchase history. The way they can track your movements to sites where you purchase products are via cookies and other bits of shared information.

So, how comprehensive is this data, you ask? It is **so** comprehensive that government agencies and law enforcement routinely ask folks like Google for your individual profile history and any other personal information you may have given them by virtue of the EULA (End User License Agreement) you agree to by using their service.

Think about that for a moment. Here we have the NSA building, a 1.5 million square foot data capture facility, to harvest phone calls, emails, searches, and anything else you may do where a signal is emitted. We have 37,000 FBI agents running about and who knows how many CIA agents.

Even with all of this brainpower, manpower, and the 65 megawatts of power at the new NSA facility, government agencies get their "personal profile" information from a public advertising engine service. That should tell you how much of your life Google stores, and sells.

You now might be asking, "How many requests are made by government entities for Google users?" Well, I'll tell you. Insofar as the data requests for a particular user, there were 21,389 in the six-month period ending on 12/31/12. That's all the data requested by that user for an undetermined amount of time.

Even worse, agencies requested specific, personal information from the actual Google account held by the user 33,634 times in the same 6-month time frame.

It doesn't take a genius to ascertain that the volumes of data Google has on you and me is far more than we may have considered, to the point Law Enforcement uses it to take some manner of legal action. That's scary stuff. I could go into the legal ramifications of a judge actually thinking that data has any evidentiary value, but we'll have to wait until later for that.

Before we tackle the problem of protecting that information, let's see exactly what data Google collects and what data they give away (or sell). According to Google's own privacy statement, they collect:

   a. User account information like name, address, credit card numbers (where applicable), pictures, and might even create a Public Profile you don't even know about.

b. What Google services you use, what web sites you view, and everything you do when looking at or clicking ads, including what specific ad it is. Cookies regarding your habits are also shared with any number of third parties. And obviously the gmail traffic you create including sending to and received from data.

c. Phone logs like your phone number, phone numbers you call, forwarded calls, duration, where and when the call was made, SMS "routing information" (whatever that means), and finally, once they figure out it is you by cross-referencing data, they will link your phone number to your Google profile.

d. Full set of information about the computer you are using, such as your hardware make and model, your OS, browser information, unique IDs of hardware, etc. This data alone can easily and uniquely identify you as a specific user. This data is then linked to your profile.

e. Many applications use Google APIs. Map location is one, music streaming another. Google logs things like your GPS location, other information from a mobile device, what WiFi areas you are in (again, including GPS location).

f. They know what applications you install or uninstall, what applications you have, how and when you use them under the auspices of "auto-update" checks in the order of four or six times per day.

You know, little stuff like that. Google does, however, say they have strict policies in place regarding the disbursement of your data. These include the provision to share all of your data with:

a. Law enforcement, government entities like the IRS or Homeland Security, or whatever agency asks and they see fit to comply with.

b. To "affiliates," businesses or people they "trust" or who say they will access the data in "good-faith," Google employees, partner companies, and that guy from Burger King who sings "ding fries are done." And my favorite (directly quoted) where they produce data, apparently to anyone, to "detect, prevent, or otherwise address fraud, security or technical issues." So if your video won't go to 1900×1200, that's a technical issue, so someone can ask for your data.

c. Other sarcasm aside, this I take quite seriously. Buried in their "we use SSL to protect you" bits, they say they also "restrict access" to "employees, contractors, and agents."

What that means is the data you thought was encrypted from end-point to end-point really isn't and they decrypt (or simple redirect an SSL end-point to standard HTTP traffic) your data and store it. Yes, that would be the data you thought was secure.

It's a "death by a thousand cuts" thing – a little bit of data here and there isn't that big of a deal. But when there are so many different sources of data for you, the accumulation of it all creates a real issue. And obviously a huge monetary stream.

I don't want to make it look like I'm singling Google out (even though I am) because there are other, albeit smaller, offenders as well. If you were not aware of it, Microsoft has been trying for a long time to make headway into the advertising industry. In my opinion it's a failed endeavor, as they have already had to write off over 6 billion dollars for the purchase of a single company to support the Ads Platform. Regardless, since they couple with Bing and other Microsoft "owned and operated" sites, their data-mining is also a source of significant concern, given you may stay logged into your Windows Live ID (WLID), or "Microsoft Account" (or whatever they may call it now), in perpetuity for mail, with third-party sites using WLID to authenticate you.

I'll give you an example of the reach this type of tracking can give. Let's say while at work you logon to a Microsoft service such as Windows Live Mail and leave that page up while doing other things. Then you go to Bing to search for something – that data is stored based on your WLID. You then search for "stereo systems" or some such and select a link to Best Buy. They store that too, as does Best Buy. Oh, all other data is stored as well, such as what work research you are doing, and the contents of any email you may send out or receive. At quitting time, you close out of everything and go home from work. After dinner, you go down to your XBox to play Forza Motorsport or something of the like. You have to log onto XBox Live to play the game, and when you do, your profile data is made available to whatever processes XBox decides they can send out. There used to be a company called Massive, which delivered targeted ads to video games. Microsoft purchased that company, so now you've got your data all tied up in a nice little bow. As you drive around the track, you see various billboards and such. As you do so, the video game makes a request to the ad tracking system for an ad to put on the billboard in the game. Your WLID is transferred to the ad delivery mechanism along with identifying information about your profile. Based on that connection, a behavioral targeting call is made and before you can even start into a turn you see a billboard ad for Kenwood Stereo Systems based on your search earlier at work. Massive actually went to the trouble of determining how much Kenwood should pay on the ad delivery, based on how long it was visible, what angle you were at when you saw it, and how much of the full ad you could have viewed.

Scary, huh? This happens billions and billions of times a day, all day, everyday, to countless numbers of other websites and data harvesters.

There are other, and in some ways greater, evils playing this game. If you were wondering, this is where I mention Facebook. Facebook is a massive "in service" ad engine, but also has a web of affiliates giving and taking your personal data. The reason Facebook has that "keep me logged in" checkbox is so they can stick to what they say their privacy policy is while also keeping that cookie alive so that all the affiliate sites you go to can get ad data from Facebook while passing back as much information as they have on you. In fact, even if you are not logged in, sites will actively create objects redirected to Facebook to contribute to the Global Fleecing.

The Emperor Has No Clothes. And Neither Do You!

Now that we're all feeling exposed by these corporate wolves, the real question is "what do we do about it?" Well, remember the previous bit about me not going into the legal ramifications? I lied. One thing we *can* do about it is to pay attention to these legal cases where Facebook or Google data is used as part of the investigation or prosecution. The data shouldn't be allowed. There is absolutely no way whatsoever the integrity of such data can be ensured. Think about the sweeping access Google can give to your information. Think about how many global outsourced contractors they have (10,000+) such as GenPact Ltd. in Bermuda and other outsourcers in other countries. Who has access to your data then? Do you trust the 30,000+ employees world-wide? You and I have no idea, and never will, how many of these people could change, add, or delete the information Google stores on us. For instance, what if one of them dumped some child pornography into your email account and then turned you in to the feds? The courts would consider this to be "solid" evidence against you because Google said it was your information. This should be brought to everyone's attention. If we allow this data to be acceptable in court, we are doomed. DOOMED, I say! OK, I'm done with that bit.

Our goal in the rest of this chapter is to limit the overall amount of data we make available on the internet and then, to the best of our ability, limit how much of that data is available for harvesters. The first step, limiting what we give out, can be applied anywhere and on any OS, but is something I consider very important.

With sites like Facebook, since more of this information is shared than we know, and even more capable of being generated, it is really important to think through what your intent of being on Facebook is. If you wish to keep in touch with friends, then make sure you make your profile private. Friends (and Facebook) will have full access, but keep it out of the public domain.

Never put your real information on Facebook if you can help it, including your name if you can. My Facebook name was a little vulgar, but since it sounded oriental (my last name was "Tang") it wasn't flagged. I said I lived in a different country, went to a different school, and was fluent in Scottish.

Your friends will know who you are, or you can tell them. It's far easier than you would think. Regarding friends, only "friend" people you actually know. If you wish to treat the number of friends you have on Facebook as a metric by which to measure your popularity or self-worth, you will do so at the cost of exposing your personal information to potentially anyone in the world. Your "friends," once you post something, can copy that data and do whatever they want with it and there is absolutely nothing you can do about it. As such, your data could be (indeed, *will* be) forever preserved on the internet for all time. So when your son or daughter (or you, for that matter) posts some picture with a blow-up doll in one hand and a bottle of whisky in the other, that image could turn up 10 years later when a prospective employer does a bit of research on you before giving an interview. Your ex-spouse could be spying on you to find out if an alimony increase is due, particularly if you post pictures of you in Jamaica with your new "friend" on a shopping spree. I once allowed myself to get into a chat-fight on Bill Maher's page with someone who was clearly wrong, and where I was obviously right.

I went to his page, and not only was it publicly available, but he had pictures of his kids with their names, and a list of cousins, aunts, and other relatives. Within a few minutes, I knew where he and his +1 lived, where they worked, what they looked like, and who their friends were. In just a few minutes, I had all manner of other information, which would have taken me significant effort to gather back in the day. Luckily for him I'm not some whack-job, but I must say the flowers I sent to him from his "Midnight Lover" probably twisted up his girlfriend a bit.

There is another process I want to highly recommend you adopt, and it regards the overall account data you use when purchasing items on the internet. I have done this myself and can't tell you how many times it has saved me considerable time while protecting my "identity" and money. While this has nothing to do with any specific operating system or application, I have to say that if everyone did this, identity theft and exposure to unauthorized transactions would drop dramatically.

There are two things I suggest you do: go get a P.O. box, and go open a debit card account at your bank that is an entirely separate account from any others you may have. Get a debit card for this account – NOT a "credit card." There is no reason to use a credit card to purchase something on the internet unless you don't have the money to pay for it and wish to make payments on items. I humbly submit that from an economic standpoint, people should not buy things they can't afford. If you can't buy a new monitor or your Macbook Pro without paying cash for them, then don't buy them online. Drive down to Best Buy or phone in the order in cases where you must use a credit card, but don't buy online with one.

I have two accounts at Chase – one is "Production" and the other "Internet." The internet account has a single debit card associated with it, and the only thing I use that account for is internet purchases. I never, ever, use my production account or any other credit card for internet purchases. The internet account was created using my P.O. box account, and I only keep about $100 in it at any given time. Right now there's $25 or so in it. It's important for you to do as I did and ensure there is NO overdraft protection on the account. I've specifically configured the account so that if there is not enough money in the account the transaction will be denied just as if you were at the ATM. In this way, you can't be charged overdraft fees.

If I wish to purchase something on the internet and don't have enough in my internet account, I simply go to Chase online banking and transfer from one account to the other. The funds are immediately available and I can make my purchase without waiting for anything.

This setup buys me a tremendous amount of protection. For one, the worst that can happen if a vendor's database is compromised and my bank information disclosed is that I lose $25 or so. They can't make any credit purchases, and they can't purchase something for more than I have in the bank. Nor can I be charged overdraft fees.

The only personal information they can possibly get from me is my special P.O. box number and not my actual address. The best thing is that I don't care in the least if my account details are released. If they are, and I see fraudulent activity, I just report it, get my money back, cancel that particular debit card and get a new one. I'm never at any level of exposure beyond what I have in that special account.

In fact, literally while I was writing this chapter, I got an email from Adobe saying they were compromised and my password information and bank account information could have been disclosed. I have a recurring payment to Adobe for Creative Cloud, so they have my internet account debit card number on file. If I were using a credit card instead, I wouldn't be writing this right now. I'd be on the phone with the bank canceling the credit card and then going through and trying to figure out where I used that card, where it may be on file, and where reoccurring transactions may be at the risk of failing and my losing service (such as Netflix and Adobe Creative Cloud) and, more importantly, I'd be worried and anxious about what exposure I may have knowing it is really outside of my control.

I honestly didn't care if that account got compromised so I just kept on writing. It's actually not even worth me canceling the account since I'm not at any financial exposure and I know every transaction on that account. That's the other benefit – the accounting on that account is crazy simple. I know there won't be any non-internet transactions on it, and know I only need look at that account for transaction details. In other words, I don't have to scour through a hundred other transactions looking for one that may have been sourced from the internet.

Now, millions of people use PayPal, but I don't anymore. At first, it was great. I just used my internet account to associate with my PayPal account. But then PayPal wanted me to get some other debit card to use just for them which would allow me to go to the ATM and withdraw funds deposited via donations at my website. I thought I'd give it a shot, but they immediately sent me an email asking for my SSN, proof of current address by way of a utility bill, and a copy of my driver's license. I wrote back saying "in that case, no thanks." But they still wanted it to keep my regular PayPal account open. I literally emailed them about 5 times saying I just wanted my regular account but they completely ignored me. So I cancelled my account.

PayPal is a risk-management company, not a bank. When companies like this start asking for people's Social Security numbers, driver's license and copies of utility bills, something very, very wrong is happening with the way we make online transactions.

This is why it is extremely important for you to take your own measures to protect your information. If you actually trust a company like PayPal to protect your core identity information, then you're simply asking for your identity to be stolen. I know that may sound harsh, but PayPal *will* be breached, and your data *will* be exposed. It's simply a matter of time.

Don't think about damage control – think about damage prevention.

SECTION TWO: TECHNICAL PRIVACY AND SECURITY – LIMITING ACCESS TO SITES

Mac OS X ships with an Apple-developed browser called *Safari*. Safari is a perfectly capable browser, and many people (I presume) are happy with everything it does. I, however, choose to use Firefox as I find it to be a superior stand-alone browser with far more configuration options available to ensure your safety and privacy. In this section, I'll be using Firefox in conjunction with an application called Little Snitch, a third-party application protocol firewall. Normally a third-party application would be part of a separate chapter regarding third party software, but I discuss it here as it directly impacts your ability to secure and control what protocols, applications, and destinations your data is bound for.

First, let's talk a little bit about Little Snitch, a for-pay firewall application developed by a company called Objective Development. While OS X does indeed come with its own firewall capabilities (covered in a different chapter) – in fact some extremely powerful and granular capabilities – I consider Little Snitch to be a requirement for any OS X installation, as its usability and power is incredible in its own right. In its most basic form, Little Snitch is an application that runs in the background, watching every outbound packet to see if its protocol type is allowed, if it is allowed to a specific destination port, and if it is allowed to any particular host, or domain. You can tell it to have "static" rules such as *deny all outbound HTTPS (port 443) traffic to doubleclick. net for all time* or *deny all outbound HTTPS (port 443) traffic from Firefox to doubleclick.net until I close Firefox. If I open it again, ask me what I want at that point.* And of course, you can have global rules such as *allow all traffic from all applications to hammerofgod.com* or *deny all traffic from any application to facebook.com* (I actually have this as a rule).

There are any number of other configurations, profiles, and rules you can leverage, but for the purposes of this chapter, I'm going to concentrate on Little Snitch's capability of asking you what behavior you wish it to take each time an unknown connection is made. Another way of saying "unknown connection" would be to say "ask each time a connection is attempted where an allow or deny rule does not already exist." Here's a shot of the Little Snitch rules interface.

In normal browsing scenarios this can actually be a bit tedious to manage for rules where you validate connections each time an application is opened, but in the following examples you see why this is important.

I'm sure most of you know this, but for those who do not, browsers offer different functionality via small files called "cookies" that each site you visit can (by default in most cases) create and store data relevant to your connection. Many, many sites use cookies to maintain persistent logon information as you move around within a site, and others are used to exchange information between sites by way of "redirects" or calls one site makes to another. Here's an example. Say you are a frequent user of Facebook. If so, you will have a cookie on your system in which facebook.com can store any manner of identifying information about you. So let's say you go to foo.com, and foo.com wants to deliver an ad to you, and is using Facebook to do so. Foo.com can't read the Facebook cookie because it is encrypted and only facebook.com can read it. But what it can do is have a small piece of code in the web-page make a separate connection to facebook.com, which can then extract its cookie, read what information it needs to deliver an advertisement to you, and then pass that data back to foo.com along with whatever data foo.com wants to collect on you, provided Facebook supplies it.

When cookies are enabled by default, this will happen in the background and you'll never see it. However, if you disable cookies for particular sites (or even better, only *enable* cookies for particular sites) it can actually affect functionality of the site if the web developers are not conscious enough to check for cookies being enabled or not. I'll give you an example of that in a bit.

In this example, we'll be using a default installation of Firefox, with Little Snitches network monitor disabled. I don't want to clutter up the book with a mass of trite screenshots for every little configuration, so I'll leave it up to you to install Little Snitch and figure that part out.

Let's fire up Firefox and go find a local store from the Verizon Wireless site at http://www.verizonwireless.com/b2c/storelocator/index.jsp. Easy enough: of course, we enter that URL and we get the full Store Locator page where I can look up a store by zip code.

However, what other connections are being made that we don't know about? It's just a simple store locator, so it can't really be all that bad, right?

Now let's turn Little Snitch's network monitor on and fire up Firefox again and see what is going on in the background when we visit http://www. verizonwireless.com/b2c/storelocator/index.jsp.

A Little Snitch confirmation window now pops up asking us if we want to allow the connection to the www.verizonwireless.com host. This is expected, of course. The default option is to apply whatever action you choose (deny or allow) to the application requesting the connection until that application quits. So in this case, if I clicked "allow," then the connection would be made, but the next time I started up Firefox and went to www.verizonwirelss. com it would ask me again. You can see the other options available in the dialog box.

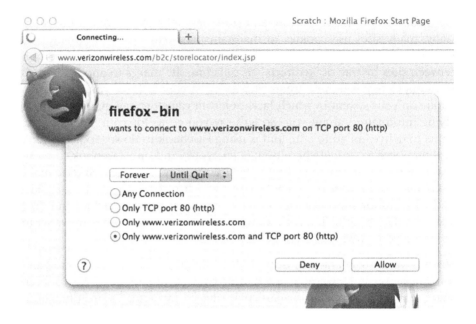

Note: in this case, the application referenced is "firefox-bin" which is the actual binary application running and not "Firefox" as you would normally see. That is because I started Firefox a bit differently, which I cover below.

I'm going to allow this connection Until Quit. Immediately after allowing this connection, I get another dialog box asking me to confirm a connection to verizonwireless.ugc.bazaarvoice.com.

And then a connection to cache.vzw.com…

And it keeps on going. And after this connection, we get a request to investor. google.com.

There is a "more information" option in Little Snitch's dialog which gives us the following text copied from it. As I continue, I'll just be providing the text and not screenshots of dialog boxes:

firefox-bin

wants to connect to **investor.google.com** on TCP port 80 (http)

IP Address	74.125.239.98
Reverse DNS Name	nuq05s01-in-f2.1e100.net
Established by	/Applications/Firefox.app/Contents/MacOS/firefox-bin
Process ID	32791
User	thor (UID: 501)

Did we ask to be directed to investor.google.com? No, we didn't. Why would we be directed to investor.google.com if all we are doing is looking for a Verizon store? Because they are all exchanging data in order to build profiles on us, or more accurately, to continue building profiles on us to target "behavioral ads" and any number of other reasons. Where else does verizonwireless.com send us? Here's a full list of redirections, in order, which we would otherwise not have known were executing in background processes:

```
firefox-bin wants to connect to seal.verisign.com on TCP port 443
(https)
firefox-bin wants to connect to b.monetate.net on TCP port 80
(http)
firefox-bin wants to connect to verizonwireless.tt.omtrdc.net on
TCP port 80 (http)
firefox-bin wants to connect to es.verizonwireless.com on TCP port
80 (http)
firefox-bin wants to connect to safebrowsing.cache.l.google.com on
TCP port 80 (http)
firefox-bin wants to connect to crl3.digicert.com on TCP port 80
(http)
firefox-bin wants to connect to crl4.digicert.com on TCP port 80
(http)
firefox-bin wants to connect to akamai.mathtag.com on TCP port 80
(http)
firefox-bin wants to connect to log.invodo.com on TCP port 80 (http
firefox-bin wants to connect to t.acxiom-online.com on TCP port 80
(http)
firefox-bin wants to connect to analytics.verizonwireless.com on
TCP port 80 (http)
firefox-bin wants to connect to tags.bkrtx.com on TCP port 80
(http)
firefox-bin wants to connect to tags.bluekai.com on TCP port 80
(http)
firefox-bin wants to connect to view.atdmt.com.nsatc.net on TCP
port 80 (http)
firefox-bin wants to connect to ads.adrdgt.com on TCP port 80
(http)
firefox-bin wants to connect to adclick.g.doubleclick.net on TCP
port 80 (http)
firefox-bin wants to connect to ads.bluelithium.com on TCP port 80
(http)
firefox-bin wants to connect to www.google.com on TCP port 80
(http)
firefox-bin wants to connect to sales.liveperson.net on TCP port 80
(http)
firefox-bin wants to connect to p.acxiom-online.com on TCP port 80
(http)
firefox-bin wants to connect to d.monetate.net on TCP port 80 (http)
```

```
firefox-bin wants to connect to gtm01.nexac.com on TCP port 80
(http)
firefox-bin wants to connect to scache.vzw.com on TCP port 443
(https)
firefox-bin wants to connect to dpm.demdex.net on TCP port 80
(http)
```

Finally, after all these connections are made, we can then look for a store. However, after we submit our request, even more connections are attempted:

```
firefox-bin wants to connect to blip.tv on TCP port 80 (http)
firefox-bin wants to connect to s.amazon-adsystem.com on TCP port
80 (http)
firefox-bin wants to connect to 20505771p.rfihub.com on TCP port 80
(http)
firefox-bin wants to connect to insight.adsrvr.org on TCP port 80
(http)
firefox-bin wants to connect to d.agkn.com on TCP port 80 (http)
firefox-bin wants to connect to action.media6degrees.com on TCP
port 80 (http)
firefox-bin wants to connect to b.collective-media.net on TCP port
80 (http)
firefox-bin wants to connect to t.brand-server.com on TCP port 80
(http)
firefox-bin wants to connect to ingest.fwmrm.net on TCP port 80
(http)
firefox-bin wants to connect to sales.liveperson.net on TCP port
443 (https)
```

What is rfinhub.com? What is media6degrees.com? And what about demdex.com? Who knows?

I'm not suggesting all of these connections are "evil," but in many (if not most) cases we have no idea what data is actually being exchanged between our browser and any given host, or what data is being exchanged between these third-party hosts by way of cookie data.

Again, this was just one simple visit to what we would have thought was a single website where we just wanted to look up any given Verizon store's location. I hope this one example will give you some level of insight into how our personal information is being violated.

To be sure, we certainly could have decided to "deny" any or all of the connection requests, but in some cases doing so breaks the website functionality. If you don't allow cookies to the Verizon site, the lookup function simply doesn't work and you won't know why. This isn't always the case, and there actually may not be any issue with a Verizon cookie in itself, but you just don't know. I've successfully blocked most ad harvesting sites altogether, but in the following Google example you can't.

When you make a submission to Google and choose a result from your search, that result is encrypted and you can only be redirected to the site you clicked if you allow your submission to be parsed by static.google.com. So you can't even use the site if you don't allow them to collect your data. I've been able to "work around" this with some copy and paste foo, but for the most part it just won't work.

This is why simply blocking all cookies isn't a very feasible option. Web sites just won't work and developers are too lazy to check if cookies are required or not. You'll find exceptions as I did with SewellDirect.com, a provider of electronic components. As you'll see in the next section, by default, browser behavior is to block all cookies. When you block cookies at SewellDirect.com, however, you'll see this:

Please enable cookies to place an order at SewellDirect.com.

Orders received by 5:00 PM EST usually ship same business day.
Packages are shipped from Orem UT, 84057

I wish other companies would provide this level of detail in your browser experience.

What we'll discuss next are some ways to better control what data is sent, and to where. We'll do this with a combination of only allowing cookies to approved sites (sites you specifically identify as trusted), as well as the complete blocking of any connection to specific sites.

Firefox "Profiles"

There's just no getting around the fact that you will have to allow connections to some sites and allow cookies to get anything done. This will be the case for your banking sites, sites you logon to for services (such as Facebook), and any other number of sites. I personally don't use Facebook in any capacity whatsoever because I know what they are doing with my data. Most people are not willing to do that though.

So let's start with sites where we need to get work done. In this section we're going to create a "profile" in Firefox allowing us to configure specific browser settings which are distinct from other profiles. For instance, my "work" profile is called `ThorProfessional` while my "don't care" profile is called `Scratch`.

The beauty of profiles is that Firefox allows you to select which one you want to use when you execute the browser binary. By default, Firefox loads with a default profile without asking you if you want to choose, create, or delete any given profile. As such, you're going to have to launch Firefox in a way that tells it to ask for a profile. This is done by directly executing the binary in Terminal (I use iTerm as discussed in Chapter 3) with a -p flag.

Rather than clicking your Firefox icon, open up a session in Terminal/iTerm and type the following:

```
/Applications/Firefox.app/Contents/MacOS/firefox-bin -p
```

This will start a new instance of Firefox with the profile manager enabled showing your "default" profile.

We're going to create a new profile – in my case, ThorProfessional – by clicking the "Create Profile" button which shows an introduction dialog box and then presents you with the create form.

Once that is created, you will see the "Choose User Profile" dialog box with the newly created profile selected. Go ahead and Start Firefox with this profile so we can begin customizing our preferences. Once you've created the profile, you can start Firefox normally and you can choose which profile to use.

Pull up the Firefox Preferences dialog box and select the Privacy icon. This is where we'll set who we will allow cookies from and other behaviors.

By default I tell all sites I do not wish to be tracked (some, of course, couldn't care less what you want) and in History I've deselected "Remember my browser and download history," "Remember search and form history," and "Accept cookies from sites." The last one is what prevents my browser from accepting any cookies from anyone. As mentioned before, this won't work with our work-related and other cookies-required sites. You'll note the "Exceptions…" button – here is a clip from the sites that I will accept cookies from.

I've got several sites in this collection, but the main point is that only these sites can ever place a cookie for my browser. This alone can be a very, very powerful way for you to prevent other sites from placing cookies and tracking your data.

You should be aware that maintaining an "allow only" process can be a bit tedious at first, but since I spend most of my time in ThorProfessional all day, it's totally worth it for me. And actually, the sites I visit in ThorProfessional almost always work with cookies turned off; it's only when I want to logon somewhere or order something that I need to add the exception for any given site. After months of using this particular profile those are the only sites with cookies on my system for `ThorProfessional`.

That's it – really! Each site can have any number of actual "cookie" files, but these are the only ones I've allowed to do so. Other places in my Exceptions list don't create persistent cookies, as they don't need to.

Understand there is a difference between what cookies you allow/deny in Firefox and the functionality provided in Little Snitch. Firefox will prevent a site you visit from dropping a cookie via your browser. Little Snitch will allow/deny access to the site in the first place.

Now that we've covered a "professional" or "limited" configuration for enabling cookies per site, let's go back and talk about the default profile. It is not feasible to only have the professional profile where you select sites you want to visit. You can certainly try it as I do, but you might want to at least give yourself the option of having a "standard" or "default" profile you can launch when you have enough work to do on sites that require cookies that you don't want to go through the hassle of setting up in your professional profile; nor should you.

You can either change the default profile to suit your requirements or of course create others. I actually have a few different profiles. In fact, in one case where I was contracted to design a security curriculum for Microsoft Azure (which I affectionately call "OhSure") I created one specific profile for work on that project because of the wide requirements Microsoft had for cookies being enabled in order for their overall service offering to function correctly. Oh, one quick bit o' trivia for you. Microsoft has named their cloud services "Azure," even though azure is the color of a cloudless sky. Go figure.

Anyway, as an example of exactly what can go on in the background on the default cookie configuration of Firefox (or any other browser for that matter) I've added a process to the Advanced Configuration section of this chapter called "Low Level Firefox Profile and Configuration Editing" which will allow you to access the database where Firefox stores cookies and configuration information. This is a *far* superior design to the Windows solution, where Internet Explorer just dumps cookies as actual files to the file system, which then must implement convoluted access controls and permissions to them and which also depends upon the System Registry (or as I call it, *The Bloated Single Point of Failure* solution) to function at all.

Regardless, the functionality illustrated here should give you rich opportunity to learn and play as you master your browser configurations to enhance your security and protect your privacy.

Alternate Search Engines

The easiest way to keep Google and Bing from harvesting your personal information is to simply not use them to search for things. I have a few alternate search engines I use which are not commercially engaged in selling your information, or even tracking it for that matter. One such search engine I use when I can is "DuckDuckGo," a privately funded search engine product which relies upon a number of different sources to provide search results. This is via API (Application Programming Interface) calls to other search engines as well as "crowdsourced" resources like Wikipedia. DuckDuckGo will make these searches for you, and return the results without tracking your information. Though it may be counterintuitive, this model ensures that all results are "equal" among users. If you go to Google and search for "Hooch Dog Diggity," your result set will be different than if I search for the same thing. To be sure, I've never searched for "Hooch Dog Diggity" before in my life because the term just popped into my head while I wrote this. But that's not the point – the point is that Google *filters* your results based on what Google thinks you want, or more accurately, based on what results Google wants you to have. The same search criteria entered into DuckDuckGo will return the same results irrespective of who requests it.

This is important to me. Honestly, I don't see how Google can get away with filtering results to specific individuals when we, for the most part, are under the assumption they actually return results based on what we asked for, not what they want to give us. What is even more concerning to me is that Google not only filters results, but that over time, the results have become purposefully reduced in relevance. This means they are "padding" results with slightly off-kilter content, which makes you visit places you wouldn't normally visit. This of course drives up ad hits as you are sent to places you thought contained the content you were looking for.

This can't happen with DuckDuckGo, and that's a good thing. However, this comes at a cost. DuckDuckGo only has a few employees and is funded by an entrepreneur who made millions on the sale of a previous venture. I like seeing people "give back" to the community that supported their endeavors. As such, they simply can't afford to spend the billions and billions Google puts into research and development, and this is reflected in the result sets. It's not that they are convoluted or inaccurate, it's just that they are not quite what we are used to with spoon-fed results (force-fed?) from Google so you have to do a bit more exploring to get the things you may want. That said, you'll also get results Google would never have given you so it's a bit of a trade-off. I use DuckDuckGo when I can, but even I must sometimes capitulate to the technical capabilities Google has and use their service. But at least we have a choice and can make decisions for ourselves. Another alternative is Privatelee which I also use, and is "Tor" friendly. I suggest you explore other options if you are concerned about your privacy. And, speaking of Tor, let's discuss what that is and what it can do for you.

TOR Proxy

Let's now talk about your IP address, which is probably the single most exploited element in the attack on your privacy. Being true to my "anti-bloat" policy, I won't go into details about what an IP address is as you can DuckDuckGo it for yourself, but I will cover it a bit.

Your IP is supposed to be a unique numerical identifier as to the Internet Protocol address you are coming from, similar to what physical address you live in. However, it doesn't actually play out that way. Your IP address and the IP address reported to web sites and lookup services can be completely different. It all depends on your provider, the time of connection you have, and the way you connect up to the internet. By way of example, I used to have a static business circuit from Comcast in my home – this means the IP address reported was always the same. This is (for the most part) required when you host your own services.

However, if you were to look up my IP address and map it back to a geographical location, it could return any router address Comcast supported as their infrastructure routing is completely different than the egress point your actual "external" IP is sourced from. So while I lived in the Seattle area, my lookup could tell you I was in Denver somewhere.

You'll see shows and movies where the almighty IP address is used to immediately identify the physical location of a bad guy, but for the most part that is simply ca-ca. If the police wanted my physical address, they would have to get it from Comcast, not some sexed-up stripper on CSI.

All that said, though your IP address won't immediately give up your physical location, it is indeed maintained as your identifying address for the purposes of logical association. It's like your cell phone – you can call someone from Seattle or Denver and the other side of the call won't know where you are, but it's still your cellphone number.

During social engineering engagements I always used a "caller ID spoofing" service to make my phone number show up differently than what it really was. I also used it to screw with my friends by calling them from their mother's phone number, which causes their cell phone to display "Mom" or whatever they've logged her number in as (assuming it is in their cell phone, of course). They'd answer and I'd proceed to tell them about my new, hot girlfriend whose house I was at right then. Good times.

With this knowledge in hand, you can see how an IP spoofing service can be valuable. Hence the introduction of a networking infrastructure called

Tor. "Tor" brings back some nice old memories of an oriental girl I used to date, as that's what she called me, but in this case it's a very powerful privacy tool.

The term "spoof" may be accurate for caller ID in that you are still calling from your phone but the displayed phone number is different, but it's actually not technically correct for Tor. I previously used the term "IP spoofing" incorrectly on purpose to support my example.

When you use Tor, you're not actually "spoofing" anything – your egress traffic actually *is* coming from a completely different system with a different IP address. Here's how it works.

Tor is an international network of privately supported "exit relays" literally located all over the world. These exit relays are supported by thousands of internal relays that route your traffic through them to an actual exit relay from which your internet connection is then sourced. The OS X Tor application is an extremely easy tool to use. When you fire it up and ask to connect to the Tor network, a list of relays is enumerated and different bandwidth, speed, and traffic algorithms are used to connect you to one of them with a secure channel. The relay you connect to will then establish a completely separate connection to another relay. The 2nd Tor relay connection is also made with a secure channel; however, the 2nd relay has no idea who you as a client are. The 2nd relay only knows about the 1st relay. At a minimum, a 3rd relay connection is made from the 2nd relay to yet another Tor relay. Again, the 3rd relay only knows about the 2nd relay. The 3rd relay does not, and cannot, even know what the 1st relay is. This can actually happen a few more times, but at least three internal relay connections will always be made. Then, finally, the last internal relay makes a secure connection to the Exit Relay from which the actual connection to the internet is made. Note that when I say the "relays" don't know anything about the traffic, that means the operators of these relays as well. Only the exit relay could monitor your traffic, and that's only if you used HTTP. Of course, this is no different than your provider or any other connection you currently make over HTTP.

As such, when you are connected to the Tor relay and wish to visit Facebook, for instance, your request is sent to the internal relay you are connected to, which is relayed to the 2nd, which is relayed to the 3rd, which is relayed to the Exit Relay that makes the actual connection to Facebook.

Now let's say you post video evidence of some cops in Kentucky beating up a pregnant woman. Of course, those officers and the agency they work for will say you have illegally recorded them without permission and will seek to charge you with a crime with a more severe sentence than rape in most jurisdictions. I'm not making that up, by the way. It's true.

Anyway, the cops go to Facebook and request full connection information on the client that posted the video in order to put the pinch on you. Fortunately, thanks to the power of Tor, the only information they can get is from the Exit Relay, which is most likely physically located in Russia, Germany, or any other country in the world.

Even if law enforcement gets some manner of international warrant for the Exit Relay to disclose what information it has, the only possible information it can give is what connection it was made from. It does not know and cannot know anything else about the connection. In this way, it is impossible to trace that post back to you as the locations of the "blind" internal relays can't be traced back anywhere. It is a thing of beauty, and a powerful tool to protect your identity.

Running Tor on your individual Mac is almost trivial. Just download the Tor OS X application and run it. You'll see this window:

Simply click "Start Tor" and the application will do the rest. As described previously the relay-to-relay connection process will execute, and before you know it you'll be exiting the Tor network and onto the internet from the other side of the world (or wherever). Once the connection is complete, Tor will launch the TorBrowser application (a Firefox instance) for you, showing you your connection information.

Congratulations. Your browser is configured to use Tor.

Please refer to the Tor website for further information about using Tor safely. You are now free to browse the Internet anonymously.

Your IP address appears to be: **212.96.58.189**

In this case, we've received the IP address of 212.96.58.189 which just happens to be in one of my favorite places:

Budapest is lovely this time of year. The identification of "No Proxy Detected" is significant – the IP lookup site I used has no idea I actually *am* using a proxy per se, but since my traffic is exiting directly from that physical relay, it thinks I'm not. And it's their business to provide accurate information.

You're ready to browse knowing your location and IP are absolutely private. Now, before you establish a permanent connection to Tor, there are a couple of things to know. First and foremost, since you are being relayed through a number of volunteer-owned systems, each with their own internet connections, the bandwidth you operate within will normally be a good bit slower than any "direct" connection through your ISP. But that's a small price to pay for ultimate anonymity. Secondly, some sites may not provide functionality if they know you are coming from the Tor network. An example of this is, you guessed it, Google. While on the Tor network, a visit to Google yields this:

Google Sorry...

We're sorry...

... but your computer or network may be sending automated queries. To protect our users, we can't process your request right now.

See Google Help for more information.

© 2009 Google - Google Home

You see, Google monitors the Tor network for exit relay IPs. They make the totally bogus claim of your network "sending automated queries" but they explicitly know you're on the Tor network and block you accordingly. They are a commercial entity, and can certainly make their own decisions about what clients they wish to serve, but in this case they figure that if they can't track you, or if they can't verify your actual IP address, that they won't let you use their service. Again, I completely respect their decision, and if I were a company who made money by selling IP profile information I very well might make the same choice, but the important takeaway is that your IP identification as part of your permanent profile is so valuable that if they can't make money off of you, they block you from their service. To be fair, this doesn't always happen. I don't think they can keep up with the Tor network in real-time, and it honestly can't be that much of a priority for them, but just be aware it could happen. If it does happen, I've been successful in bypassing the block by directly visiting the localized Google service, in this case www. google.hu. When you do this, you'll obviously have to change the local language to English.

Advanced Configuration Example: Low Level Firefox Profile and Configuration Editing

As mentioned before, Windows applications of any consequence rely and are dependent upon the use of the System Registry to store application data. The System Registry is a shared repository, or as they call it a "database" of extremely complex and convoluted objects and elements. As a shared resource, if the registry gets corrupted or otherwise damaged, all programs dependent upon it will cease to function. The fact than any program you install reads and writes to the Registry means that program could potentially render the Registry inoperable. Microsoft plays down the risk of this happening, but it's easy to do. Trust me, I know – I've done it many, many times (for fun, of course).

OS X applications are actually "packages," which are a physical collection of binaries and support files contained within a directory structure and protected by default restrictions and whatever additional access controls you decide to place upon them.

In the case of Firefox, the applications required files exist in two places: the main Firefox "package," and supporting files in your home directory's ~/Library/Application Support/Firefox directory. The bits we're looking for are the files contained in the directories specifically created for each profile we've created in Firefox.

I've been using a profile called "Scratch" for my general profile used for dirty browsing. No, not "dirty" like that, dirty like "unclean" and "cesspool-eo" browsing. When I created the Scratch profile, Firefox appended the name with a randomized nomenclature and built the necessary support files as follows:

▼ 🗄 Firefox
  ▶ 🗄 Crash Reports
  ▼ 🗄 Profiles
    ▶ 🗄 5vbi4n06.default
    ▶ 🗄 6440mqq7.Tor
    ▶ 🗄 pb11zaer.Thor.Professional
    ▼ 🗄 pka42g3d.Scratch
      ▶ 🗄 bookmarkbackups
      ▶ 🗄 extensions
      ▶ 🗄 healthreport
      ▶ 🗄 indexedDB
      ▶ 🗄 minidumps
      ▶ 🗄 safebrowsing
      ▶ 🗄 webapps
      📄 cert_override.txt
      📄 compatibility.ini
      📄 extensions.ini
      📄 prefs.js
      📄 sessionstore.js
      📄 urlclassifierkey3.txt
      📄 cert8.db
      📄 key3.db
      📄 secmod.db
      📄 _CACHE_CLEAN_
      📄 addons.sqlite
      📄 content-prefs.sqlite
      📄 cookies.sqlite
      📄 downloads.sqlite
      📄 extensions.sqlite

Earlier in the general Firefox section of this chapter I discussed the minimal cookies afforded to us by a customized profile. For the purposes of this section, I want to show you what a dirty profile yields insofar as cookies are concerned. In addition to the pka42g3d.Scratch direction highlighted, you note the "cookies.sqlite" file. SQLite is a "server-less," in-process Structured Query Language (SQL) process allowing any program to store and manage data in a self-contained environment. Most SQL engines require a separate "server" process, which supports a client's requirements. However, SQLite is a standalone process, which doesn't require any other process to support its functionality. The great thing about SQLite is that it is free for use in any way you wish to use it; you may include it in private applications, public applications, commercial applications, or whatever else you want to do with it. It is also "open-source" in that the source code is readily available for download. This ensures there are no secrets in the code and that everyone is freely able to examine, first hand, the exact operational components of the application.

Firefox utilizes SQLite to store and retrieve data elements in order to provide its functionality, including the creation and access of cookie data. This section is two-fold: one, to show you the power you have in accessing Firefox data elements via the SQLite, and secondly to show you exactly how much crap is dumped on you when dirty browsing.

First you'll need to download the SQLite Manager, which is not included in the default Firefox installation. This is super-easy; just go to Tools->Add-ons. Look for SQLite in the search field and install it. There's a "restart" button you need to click, and upon doing so you'll see the SQLite Manager is now available under the Tools menu.

What we'll do now is launch the SQLite Manager and open the cookies.sqlite file and see what manner of nastiness we'll find lurking there. The quickest and most efficient way to do this is to click the "open file" icon and then use the OS X "Go To Folder" feature shortcut ⇧⌘G and directly access the ~/Library/Application Support/Firefox/Profiles directory. Drill down to the profile directory you wish to examine and select the cookies.sqlite file. The Structure tab is selected by default, showing the Master Table structure. Select moz_cookies under Tables.

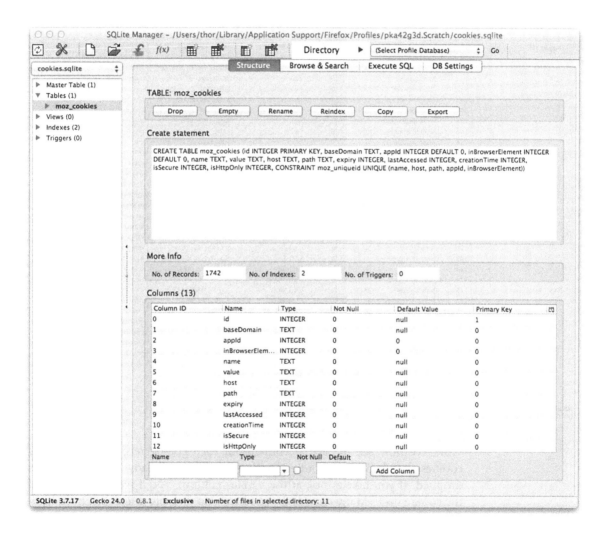

We now see the entire cookies database structure, which is really quite cool. You can't do anything remotely close to this in Internet Explorer, by the way. Now, let's select Browse & Search and see what we've got.

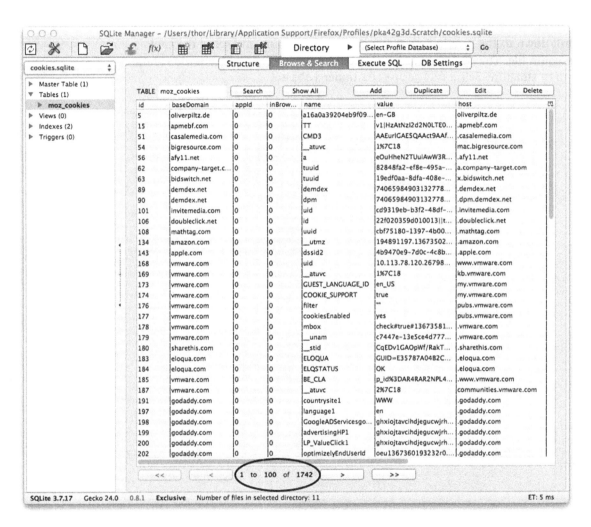

Wow. We now see the actual contents of each cookie record. I cleared my cookies on this profile about a month ago, and I've already got 1742 cookies dropped. If you take a look at the `value` column, you'll see the contents of the cookie itself. Many records down in my cookie table is a record from hub-pages.com. I've never gone to hubpages.com, but I did look about for some information on organic cereals in order to research the chemical composition of various products. I'm starting up an organic farm called Thorganics and this is of great interest to me (seriously). Somehow or another this hubpages.

com site was transferred as part of a Bing search for "organic" and "popular breakfast cereals." The really interesting thing here is that I specifically used Google to search for research sites. I purposefully never use Bing in the profile because I want to see exactly the extent of needle-sharing these sites engage in. Some site picked up my Google search by way of a referral, and that site then decided to fire off that search to Bing. hubpages.com apparently decided to transfer search authority over to Bing instead, and then dropped a cookie on my system so that any other site who wants to use hubpages.com to extract available information can do so via a redirect. The actual contents are:

```
209211014.1368496131.1.1.utmcsr=bing|utmccn=(organic)|utmcmd=organic
|utmctr=popular%20breakfast%20cereals
```

Oddly enough, further down is a cookie from ranker.com, which has this as the contents of the cookie:

```
51811754.1368496147.1.1.utmcsr=bing|utmccn=(organic)|utmcmd=organic
|utmctr=popular%20breakfast%20cereals
```

WOW! Talk about a coincidence! As you can see, both companies have their own identifier for me, yet both have the exact same information for the search criteria. I guess it's a good thing I didn't search for "Christina Hendricks' Bra Size," huh? Oh, wait...

When surfing dirty you have no idea what information is being encoded, such as lifehacker.com's `f5ptmd6egfelt9r1.1367875279554. 1367875279554.00000000000001` cookie value. Only they know what those characters all mean. Hopefully this will give you some idea of what's going on when you browse, and the importance of leveraging the procedures covered in the general Firefox Profiles section.

Advanced+ Configuration Example: Shared Tor Proxy in Virtual DMZ Environment

I'm calling this section "Advanced +" because, well, it is. There are professional engineers who can't do this, and some who don't even know it's possible. Regardless, the reason I'm in this business is because I am continually fascinated by what I learn on a daily basis, and it is one of the true, authentic joys I have. As such, I'm not going to assume that since this book is targeted at a much wider audience than I normally write for, I should further assume you won't have any interest in what we're about to talk about. If only 1% of the people reading this have a creative spark struck by this chapter, then it was worth my time. That said, even if you don't plan on implementing this, I think you should give it a read just to see what your possibilities are.

We've previously discussed installing Tor on a client-by-client basis for anonymizing various protocol traffic. What that means is each client we install Tor on (such as your laptop, your work machine, your spouse's system, etc.) will make their own connection directly to the Tor network, with each system's internet egress exiting out of a different exit node. Now, let's engineer a more advanced configuration where we will build a DMZ segment (meaning "demilitarized zone" though I am loathe to continue supporting the term) using a free and remarkable product from VMware called ESXi. Let me qualify what "free" means in this context. The ESXi server product is indeed free. However, the enterprise tools and server components to run ESXi in a production environment are actually quite expensive, but totally worth it for any given company relying on virtualization technologies.

This chapter isn't just about a Tor proxy – in fact, that just happens to be the service we will be deploying. The *real* value of this chapter is that it will show you how to create a far more secure DMZ segment for you to deploy whatever services you want to deploy. So as you read on, keep in the back of your mind the fact the functionality described herein extends far, far beyond the provisioning of a proxy.

Once we've built the DMZ, we will launch and configure an OS X virtual instance to act as our Tor proxy server *and* Tor relay. When we installed Tor on individual machines, the Tor Browser was configured to connect to the machine's local loopback address of 127.0.0.1, in order to then pipe SOCKS requests out of the outbound Tor connection from the IP address bound to your ethernet card.

In this case, we will start up Tor the same way as we did on clients on our DMZ OS X box, but change its configuration from listening on the loopback 127.0.0.1, where only *it* could connect, to instead configure Tor to listen on the IP address bound to the NIC itself (which in the example will be 192.168.2.50). Diagrams follow, but I want to make sure I properly cover the concepts in text first. In this way, all of your client machines can connect directly to the DMZ Tor box for outbound Tor browsing simply by changing the SOCKS proxy in Firefox and not installing Tor on them all. This does two things: one, you don't have to install Tor on your clients at all in favor of a common proxy, and two, you aren't making multiple connections to the Tor network but rather sharing just one.

Secondly, we will configure the DMZ OS X Tor machine to be a Bridge Relay (also described as an "internal relay") so we can become part of the overall community protecting freedom and privacy by allowing the DMX OS X Tor box to act as an intermediary between other Tor boxes as the traffic makes its way to the Exit Relay. I've configured my Tor installation as an actual Exit Relay. That's where the traffic finally exits to make the direct connection to the web site or mail server. As such, some consider running an Exit Relay can be "risky" in a sense, because certain law enforcement agencies could be obtuse and think you are up to something shady if you support Tor exit relays. I'll leave that for you to research and get on with this configuration.

ESXi is a virtualization platform where you create a dedicated host machine capable of running as many virtual machines as your hardware configuration allows, and then some. It is quite amazing what products VMware has produced, and ESXi is at the core. If you use HyperV at the moment, as far as migrating to ESXi VMs is concerned, there's really not much to talk about. You simply can't run OS X VMs on Hyper-V. That said, if you hack OS X up enough until it looks like POS X, then you might be able to, but that's true with anything. That said, if you do have existing Microsoft Hyper-V machines, VMware will easily convert them to either VMware Desktop or the ESXi VM format where you can simply add them to your ESXi inventory and be on your way. Microsoft Hyper-V is nice for a few VMs here and there – I used it myself for years. But even Microsoft doesn't use it in production where it "counts." However, they do market it as a production-class platform, but I don't understand why. There's really no comparison to ESXi, which is indeed a "true" enterprise product. That's why we're using it here. But enough of that...

So let's get started. I'm glad you've read this far in the Advanced section of the chapter as this will be quite cool. While I'd love to start at configuring the ESXi server for this bit, I must be true to the book and push through to the part where OS X comes into the picture. Actually, even if you don't plan to do this, I think you might enjoy the processes covered herein.

We will need to cover some rather extensive ESXi configuration options first, so expect some priming here. Again, as this is the only host-based virtualization product that allows you to run OS X, it's very good for you to learn about it, though it will be somewhat complicated.

To give you some context, the soon-to-follow Diagram 1.1 is a quick look at my overall ESXi deployment, consisting of 2 (two) ESXi servers, each with their own set of virtual machines.

One quick note though – this is a screenshot from the vCenter product which is a for-purchase application (and not a cheap one either). However, for the most part the view is the same as the free client software you'll use to connect, named vSphere. The difference is vCenter shows all servers and offers advanced configurations while the use of the vSphere product, being directly connected to the ESXi host (as opposed to connecting to the vCenter host/ guest) only allows you to connect to one host at a time; but this should be more than enough for your network. It is important to note this setup is running on Mac Minis which make great ESXi servers. The real added bonus is you are licensed to run as many OS X images as you wish on Mac equipment. Why have one OS X box when you can have five??

The topology I'm describing is my actual production setup. If we were using the vendor-speak so prevalent in today's market, we would call this my "Private Cloud." A Private Cloud is a collection of virtual machines you already have set up. It's what we called our "LAN with Virtual Machines" before marketing people got hold of it. However, in order for you to buy what you already have, they call it "Private Cloud" so you feel like you're on the cutting edge of stuff you've had for years.

You've probably noticed other sources and sites showing screenshots where they've obfuscated computer names and internal IP addresses. This is a silly practice. It's unfortunate because it shows these authors don't know much about security. Knowing the names of my servers or their internal IP addresses gives no valuable information to an attacker. Redacting portions of the data by way of blocks or blurs only serves to confuse people. And in most examples and test setups this sort of thing hides important components. So what you see here is all live. How's that for trust?

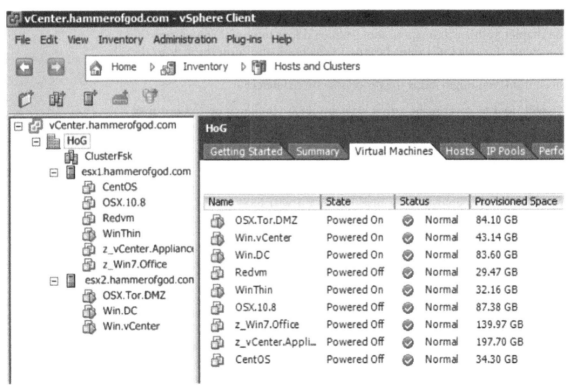

DIAGRAM 1.1

The two ESXi servers are named, originally and creatively enough, ESX.1 and ESX.2. I know. It's a gift. My testing and utility VMs are on ESX.1, and the OS X VM we'll be using for a Tor relay and proxy is on ESX.2. You'll notice I also have my vCenter vm and my Windows domain controller system on ESX.2 as well. The first thing that may pop into your mind is "You, sir, are crazy! How can you deploy of all things a Tor server on the same ESXi host where your domain controller and vCenter server lives? It's madness!!" Excellent question and concern, and I'm here to show you how I can do so and still sleep at night, albeit with assistance from Trazodone.

Diagram 1.1 shows a datacenter named "HoG," a cluster named "ClusterFsk," the ESX.1 host and its VMs, and finally the ESX.2 host and its VMs. This will be the main interface you will use to manage your VMs. This image reflects a "flat network" configuration, meaning all IPs assigned to hosts, guests, and management interfaces are on the same network; in this case, it is 192.168.1.0/24 (or 255.255.255.0, if that is your preferred nomenclature). These machines all live in the same network, and all have only outbound access to the internet.

There are no existing inbound connections being made to this network, or what one may call "port forwarding" from your ISP's "modem" or router. After we go over this diagram we'll no longer need to refer to ESX.1, as all ESX.1 assets in this example will stay on the 192.168.1.0/24 network without changing configuration. ESX.2, however, will indeed be changed.

The network topology in Diagram 1.2 represents where we will be at the *conclusion* of this chapter as it regards the ESXi configuration.

The typical home or small business network consists of workstations plugged into some manner of switch, with that switch being subsequently plugged into a router or what some vendors call a "modem." In many cases the term is inaccurate as digital-only transfers are very common. If one has tendencies toward pedanticism, the term "routing modem" may be appropriate for you. Additionally, your router probably has switch components built into it, typically designed with a small number of ethernet ports (4 or so) for the "LAN" and 1 port for "WAN" or "Internet." I've a Comcast Business Router which actually has the RG58 cable port directly integrated. Lastly, most recent routers support either a dedicated DMZ port, or allow for such functionality via configuration. My Netgear actually has both.

Your internal network's LAN IP addresses will be RFC1918 addresses, meaning they are considered "private" and nonroutable outside your network (e.g. the Internet). You'll have at least one "external" IP address provisioned by your provider.

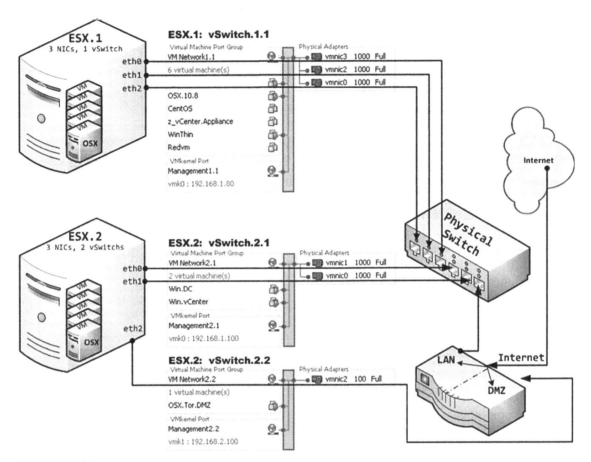

DIAGRAM 1.2

My network is probably a bit more complex and scaled higher than most home networks (and even some businesses) but my configuration is essentially the same as described. The www.hammerofgod.com external address is 173.190.165.173. I've other static IPs available but that's my primary one. All of my internal machines, other than what we're about to change, are in the 192.168.1.0/24 network and exit via the 173.190.165.173 address.

At this point, as we continue with configuring ESXi, things may get more confusing, as what are normally hardware components will now become virtualized components. Regarding Diagram 1.2, consider the initial vCenter Diagram 1.1 where we showed the "flat network," primarily the fact that all switches, NICs, hosts, and VMs were internal on 192.168.1.0 /24. With that in mind, let's focus on the network portion of our goal.

Diagram 1.2 shows two physical servers, each with five virtual OS X machines. You can already feel the power at your command!! Each host has three physical NICs. The first concept for us to cover is that of the "virtual switch." The *physical* NICs are plugged directly into the *physical* switch. However, the NICs themselves are *not* assigned IP addresses as one would typically do in a nonvirtualized environment. Well, to be specific, in a non-ESXi virtualized environment. It's counterintuitive, I know, particularly if coming from a MSFT background, but for now let's consider them "raw" physical ethernet connections with no protocols bound to them at all. In fact, wholly distinct from Windows virtualization products, ESXi *never* actually assigns IPs to NICs. This actually provides unparalleled functionality in redundancy, teaming, and failover. All communication is handled by an object called a "virtual switch" or vSwitch. The only time an IP is bound to an object is when what is called a "vKernel" port group is configured. Don't let that part throw you – I'll explain it in a bit.

Those three NICs on ESX.1 are part of a single vSwitch which manages all traffic for the VMs as well as connectivity requirements for managing different aspects of the ESX.1 host. Potentially as important, the vSwitch uses those three physical NICs to manage failover or load balancing. All IP traffic which has to do with ESX.1 and its hosts is done through vSwitch.1.1, shown in Diagram 1.3.

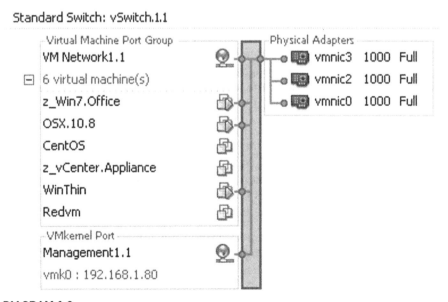

DIAGRAM 1.3

This functionality is provided by out-of-the box ESXi features without dependencies on drivers or "supported NICs" for performance or redundancy functionality. In contrast, Hyper-V is 100% dependent on your NIC manufacturer's 3rd party drivers to function in Windows. Hyper-V is also 100% dependent on the 3rd party driver's binding of the IP address directly to the NIC or team. As such, MSFT will never have these ESXi features because Hyper-V is dependent upon how the base OS works with respect to IPs and binding. Hyper-V simply has no control over it. The Windows development group will never, ever change the way the Windows kernel works in this regard. They can't, technically or otherwise. And this is what will keep Hyper-V out of the "enterprise" market (among many other things) in my ever so humble opinion. So congratulate yourself on already being ahead of the game!

OK – this is how the overall vSwitch works, and it's important for our success that we all understand it. First, Diagram 1.3 shows a preview of what a vSwitch object looks like – we'll get into much more detail in a bit:

When we create a vSwitch, which we will walk through, it is basically a "container" for other networking objects. It is told how many virtual ports exist to support a given number of virtual machines, what MTU we wish to use (typically 1500, but vSwitches support jumbo-frames as well), and it is told which physical NICs are committed to it. However, the switch knows nothing of IP address or other machine traits, other than MAC address in the same way a physical switch wouldn't. Once it knows how many NICs are at its disposal, you can configure it to use those NICs for load balancing, failover, or both at the actual *switch* level, not at the software driver level as Windows requires. Remarkably enough, you can use all three NICs for either feature, or both features *at the same time*! You can even mix and match at will: two NICs for failover, three NICs for performance. So you can literally stuff the host with NICs (not on the MacMini though), and tell the switch all are available for failover and load balancing at the same time! All Windows drivers I've seen only allow one or the other. And I hate having a perfectly good NIC just sitting there doing nothing waiting on the other to fail. But wait! There's more!

In order to use the switch for communication among other hosts, guests, and network objects about your LAN, you must create a group of ports the Virtual Machines will "virtually" plug into called a Virtual Machine Port Group. The vSwitch automatically provisions the needed "ports" from the number available via its configuration.

But check this out – you also do not give the Virtual Machine port group any IP information. That's right: though all the VMs on this port group communicate by merit of their assignment to the port group over TCP/IP, the port group itself doesn't care about IP addresses; this is much in the same way that a group of ports on a physical switch doesn't recognize IP addresses, a counterintuitive configuration for actual virtual ports. The way the NICs are provided their Observed IP Ranges is simply by tagging traffic on the wire. No muss, no fuss. Again, more on that in a moment.

As with the vSwitch, you can configure individual failover and load balancing options specifically for the VM port group. Meaning as the vSwitch has teaming, so does the Virtual Machine port group using the *same* NICs if desired. That's *major* flexibility.

The other type of port group the vSwitch supports is called a "vKernel" port group, as shown back in Diagram 1.3 we saw earlier. You will obviously need to connect up to the ESXi box to manage it, and that is via the vKernel port group. This *is* where you give the vKernel port group an IP address. The default group is set up during installation, so when you fire up the vSphere client and connect to the IP address of your ESX box, you'll connect to the IP address(s) given to vKernel ports.

The vKernel port group is also where one may configure advanced options within ESXi such as direct iSCSI support, a service called "vMotion" which moves VMs about hosts for you based on utilization and availability, and even other file system support such as NFS.

So to create our DMZ segment, we'll make a vSwitch, create a Virtual Machine port group and a vKernel port group on ESX.2 and we'll be good to go!

We'll move on by way of comparison of our persistent ESX.1 configuration and our ESX.2 final configuration, which looks like Diagram 1.4:

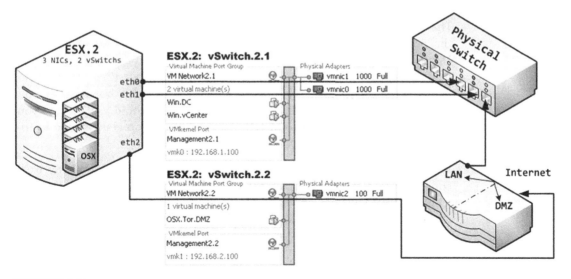

DIAGRAM 1.4

Looking at Diagram 1.2 again, we'll see ESX.1 has three NICs. The physical NICs are represented as *eth0*, *eth1*, and *eth2* though ESXi grabs them and names them *vmnic0*, *vmnic2*, and *vmnic3* as seen in Diagram 1.3. What Diagram 1.3 is actually meant to show is an "out of the box" configuration with the NICs assigned to ESX.1's vSwitch.1.1. The "observed IP ranges" shows the IP of my personal, custom built OS X rig.

To reiterate, I never had to install a single driver – ESXi bound to them natively just by plugging them in. Oh – now is probably a good time to tell you the virtual switch names are *automatically created* with very boring appellations such as vSwitch0 and vSwitch1. I explicitly renamed mine as you see in the illustrations. I like my nomenclature better as the name "vSwitch.1.1" tells me it's the first switch on the ESX.1 server; vSwitch.2.2 tells me it's the second switch on the ESX.2 host. I use this convention with "Virtual Machine" and "vKernel" port group names as well. Unfortunately, vSwitches can't be renamed in the GUI so you'll have to directly SSH into the ESXi host and edit the "/etc/vmware/esx. conf" file with "vi." I'd love to get into that, but it's way outside scope and my editor will yell at me. It's easily found on the Internet, but email me if you can't find it. So as you follow along at home, please keep this in mind.

All three NICs are assigned to vSwitch1.1. The three NICs are plugged into the *hardware* switch, and the vSwitch instance has a "Virtual Machine" port group named "VM Network1.1," and a vKernel port group named "Management1.1." As you see (still referencing Diagram 1.3) Management 1.1 has been given the IP address of 192.168.1.80; this is the IP we use to manage the host itself. Again, this IP has nothing to do with the IP ranges our VM switch observes – it's just to manage the ESXi box itself.

The "VM Network1.1" port group is where the VMs are assigned. Again, the port group itself doesn't have an IP address. I call the vKernel port "Management1.1" because it's actually how I connect to the ESXi machine to *manage* it. That's what that port group is for – to manage the host and configured vMotion, iSCSI, etc. I know I repeat this a good bit, but this was a bit chewy for me to get a grip on initially, so I thought I would explain it to you the way I had to explain it to myself – because repetition is the key to learning! Repetition is the key to learning!

With that background we'll start getting into the meat of things. Later we'll concentrate on the logic represented in the ESX.2 portion of the diagram, which is what you've been waiting for, but first we'll engage in a top-to-bottom overview with what we know so far.

Having a "flat" network doesn't prevent us from building a Tor OS X VM and making it externally available as a relay. We can always port-forward from our router to the 192.168.1.0/24 network, and we'd be done by now. However, we don't know how secure Tor is from an engineering standpoint. We have no idea under what circumstances someone might be able to breach Tor and gain access to our server or network. The same is true of Exchange, IIS, SQL Server, SharePoint, etc. etc. But we'd like to think as business-level applications they have been deeply and extensively scrutinized by many more eyes than an app like Tor. Raise your hand if you laughed.

We also don't know what sort of traffic could be routed through our relay or what manner of twisted and depraved perversions Windows Security MVPs may be engaged in while using our relay.

As such, we're going to take what we already have and, with some reconfiguration, create an isolated network segment earlier called a "DMZ" where compromise of a machine will be strictly limited in its scope of attack options to only those machines contained within that segment. Unfortunately, many have used the term DMZ to describe a network segment where sacrificial lambs and the organization's network scourge are sent to die a slow and lonely death within a maelstrom of filthy internet packets. One shudders.

Unfortunately for those businesses, a DMZ is actually the opposite. We won't dump whatever servers we want willy-nilly without a care for security thinking we've somehow protected ourselves by just putting them there. Rather, our DMZ will be forged with intention – a vision of a pristine, gleaming network paradise where every bit of traffic can be accounted for. Where no packet will be left behind!

The DMZ is where sensitive servers, generally those accepting some manner of anonymous traffic (such as web and mail) are located so that a breach of said machine – given its exposure to external and unqualified traffic – will not afford the attacker a launching pad from which attacks against the internal network can be easily launched. DMZ assets should be on a separate segment and IP space so other targets are not immediately made available in such circumstances.

This is why the DMZ should be an environment of specifically located services where any traffic can be immediately verified as valid. Internal networks are a veritable sandstorm of traffic where one packet cannot effectively be identified from another. While some folks think Intrusion Detection Systems (IDS) have some value within an internal network, I rate them at a zero insofar as use and value are concerned. That's why we will have a shiny DMZ so that we will always know if something sketchy is afoot and bad traffic will stand out like an Emu at the symphony.

There are several ways to deploy a DMZ, from routers with multiple interfaces to virtual deployments, to firewalls, to barbed-wire ethernet cables. For simplicity's stake, we'll be moving forward with the assumption our "cable-modem" or router offers this functionality. I've not seen a recent router without this feature. That part's easy enough – so let's assume you've set up your cable modem for a DMZ port. With that said, I certainly don't want to leave others in the cold if you don't have the functionality to set up a DMZ port – there will be another configuration for you to use your normal router and ESXi to make your DMZ.

With my network, the DMZ segment will have the 192.168.2.0/24 IP address space (remembering our internal network is 192.168.1.0/24). Now, it's time for you to do some work. Again, assuming you started with the flat network configuration with your base ESXi installation (which was hopefully easy), the ESX.2 diagram is where it starts for you. Oh, if you are indeed having trouble with ESXi, there are many references on the Internet. However, seeing as how VMware documentation can be a bit fragmented, if you really need assistance just fire off an email to me and I'll see if I can help. I'll do my best to respond in a valuable way.

To move forward, you are going to need at least two NICs in your ESXi box. In fact, as we move forward consider the two ESX.2 vSwitch.2.1 adapters to be one as they will be configured for load balancing that switch. If you are using a MacMini for your ESXi box, then you can buy little USB Ethernet adapters or the Thunderbolt Ethernet adapters; they'll work perfectly. An external USB/Thunderbolt will be the one we use for the DMZ as it will be plenty fast enough as we utilize the gigabit interface(s) for internal traffic.

I guess I should say you can also build your own ESXi box with commodity hardware and *still run OS X VMs*, but that would require me telling you secrets you can already get on the internet. It would also violate your Apple license agreement. And none of us would ever consider doing that, right? Hey, I don't judge, I just make sure you know what technical options you have.

A good way to look at this is that both ESX.1 and ESX.2 were identically configured before these changes. So feel free to use ESX.1 as a base reference as its configuration will not change.

At this point, all three NICs in ESX.2 are physically plugged into the physical switch. Now is probably a good time to go back and study the diagrams provided thus far. We'll leave it this way until we complete the first step, which is to change our virtual switch configuration. I prefer to leave the NIC we're about to seize plugged into the internal network while this happens, just so any misconfiguration won't lead to a problem within the DMZ.

Leaving ESX.2 vSwitch.2.1 alone, we are going to create a new virtual switch and call it, oh, I don't know, vSwitch.2.2! How original! The purpose of vSwitch.2.2 is to configure the requirements for our *physically* different DMZ network segment. This will give us ESX.2 vSwitch.2.1 serving our main 192.168.1.0/24 network and our vSwitch.2.2 switch serving resources in the DMZ. For now, we'll only have our OS X Tor machine in the DMZ.

This is done by using the Add Network Wizard as described shortly.

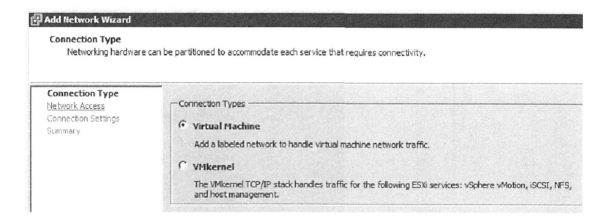

Now is where I tell you how all this work you are doing is going to pay off "x" fold in that you'll be able to spin-up virtual instances in the DMZ in a matter of minutes when you want to locate a server isolated from the internal network. The DMZ is a perfect place for you to put your new Apache web server as well by way of OS X Server. Of course, you'll have to save up for that as it costs a whopping $19.99. But it is still just a *tad* cheaper than the thousands you'll pay for a Windows Server license. Bonus!

It may be counterintuitive, but when creating a switch, the first object required is a network access port group. When that is selected, you can then get on with the rest of the process.

The "Add Networking" function brings up the previous dialog box. I'll move on and create a "Virtual Machine" port group, but you just as easily could have created a vKernel group. As previously mentioned, ESXi will now prompt me to either create a new unconfigured vSwitch or bring this network object to a different, already configured *vSwitch* as distinct from an already existing NIC. You can't do that here – you select an entire switch, or create a new one.

And now the new vSwitch configuration where we choose "create" at which point we'll go back and steal the NIC we need for it. The Add Network wizard displays this:

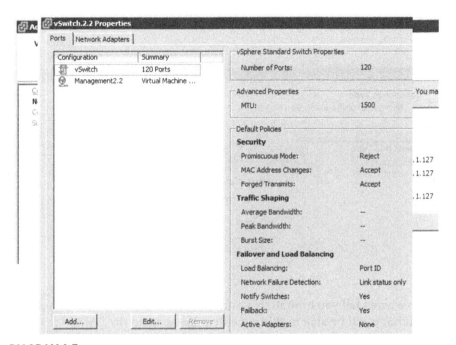

DIAGRAM 1.5

Both "Virtual Machine" and "vKernel" port group names follow the nomenclature of the ESXi hosts and vSwitches. All "vKernel" port groups on all ESXi
hosts are named Management1.1, Management1.2, 2.1, and now 2.2.

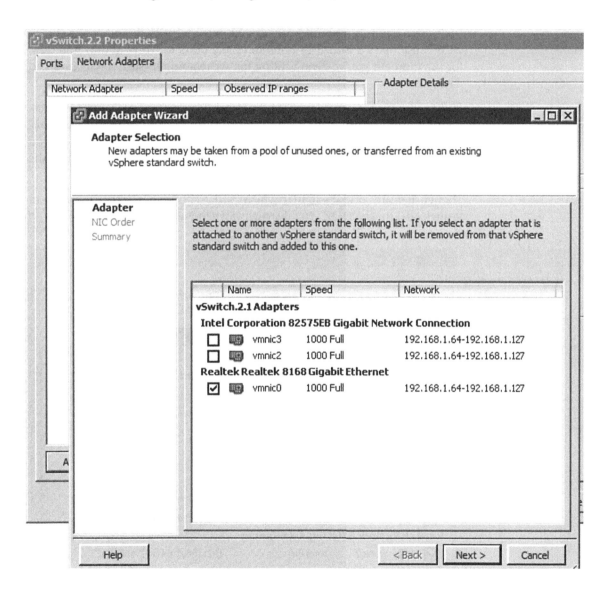

It seems a bit odd to me that the "vSwitch" configuration comes in-between the port group-type and the port group-settings, but, hey, what can you do? So you'll notice in the preview you're about to create a Virtual Machine Port Group assigned to nothing, as we've not seized an adapter yet.

I left the default number of ports to 120, but I went back and changed it to 24 because that's a bunch of unused, lonely ports to worry about. And now, for the moment you've been waiting for, we're going to steal a NIC in broad daylight!

Pull up the new (what is probably) vSwitch0 properties. As I said, the illustration shows my vSwitch after I renamed it, as do the subsequent diagrams. Select the "Network Adapters" tab, and then click "Add." This is where you can select individual NICs as opposed to vSwitches at the beginning of the Add Networking Wizard.

Though it really doesn't matter which card I choose, I selected the built-in Realtek NIC for the DMZ virtual switch vSwitch.2.2.

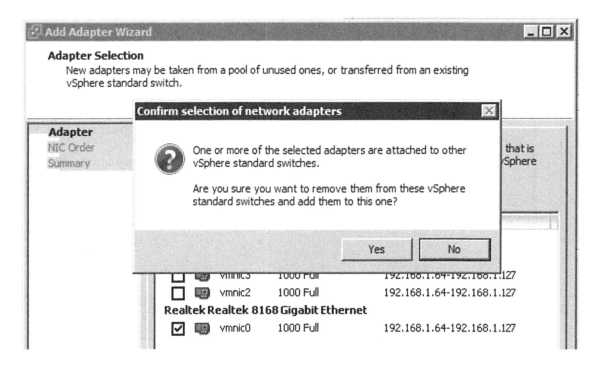

There's no particular reason to select the "odd" one as opposed any either of the other two from the dual-NIC, but after years of working with Windows trying to have some manner of decent fail-over for NICs, I'm used to binding multi-port NIC interfaces together and keeping them that way. Only the same-vendor, same-model, same-card config worked with any semblance of planned design. So I'm just going to keep the dual-port ethernet NICs together, so they stay happy. Besides, if I stole one of those guys, the other one would pine and cry, whining with Broadcast Packets, so it's best to keep the LAN quiet.

Pursuant to that point, here's the confirmation request asking if we are willing to break up the happy home of NICs currently gathered up unto ESX.2 vSwitch.2.1. Are we willing? Oh yeah, we're willing.

Let's do a quick review, and make sure we're all caught up to this point. ESX.2 used to have a single vSwitch consisting of a "Virtual Machine" port group and a "vKernel" port group. In order to reduce confusion between the Virtual Machine port group and the vKernel port group, I named all vKernel port groups "Management" with the appropriate suffix to represent the server and vSwitch number. The vKernel port group used to live in the 192.168.1.0/24 network. Three of three NICs were bound to this virtual switch, all physically connected to our main internal switch. Everything worked, and life was good. Now, in order to create the DMZ segment, we've created a new vSwitch on ESX.2 called vSwitch.2.2. We created a "Virtual Network" port group called "DMZ," and took the Realtek NIC away from vSwitch.2.1 and bound it to vSwitch.2.2 instead. We're almost through with this part of the work!

It's rather important you are up to speed, as the next section might be a bit confusing. So go ahead and review on your own. I'll wait.

Oh good! You're back!

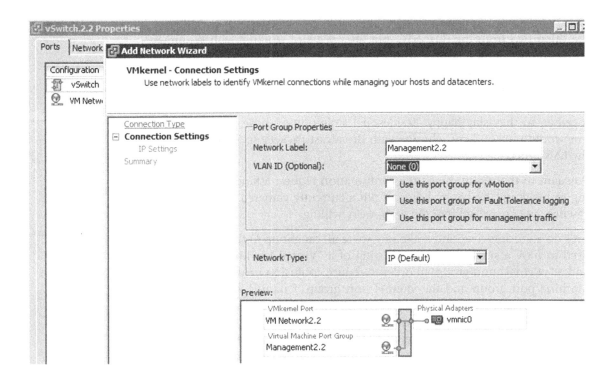

On the vSwitch2.2 I created both a Virtual Machine port group and a vKernel port group. Creating vKernel network for the DMZ is not required, and best practices would dictate you don't create one as there should be no need to perform actual management functions on ESX.2 from the DMZ. That should be done on the more secure, isolated internal network segment.

However, in my case I have a need for it (given the number of VMs I have in the DMZ) so I'll go ahead and create a Management group without actually binding management protocols to it. In this way, I can bind protocols as needed without having to interrupt operations by reconfiguring a switch while my VMs are running.

This basically creates a vKernel port group that doesn't really do anything insofar as any advanced ESXi protocols or services are concerned. Again, this is on purpose – this is our DMZ segment, and if any DMZ assets are compromised, various and sundry traffic and services could be leveraged to strengthen an attack. Given how rich management protocols are on ESXi, I'm disabling them to minimize my exposure.

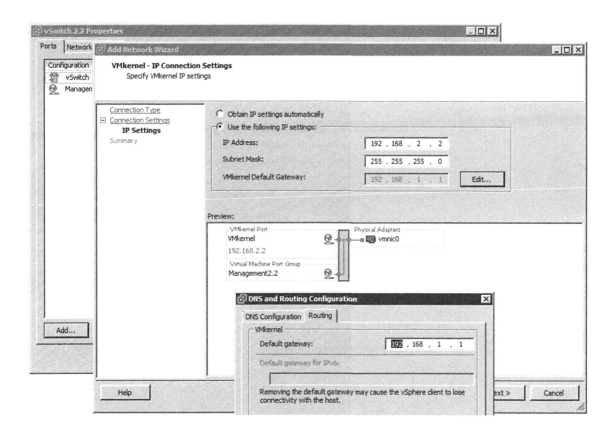

What the vKernel port group *does* do is to provide me with TCP/IP access to ESXi host-level functionality such as SSH and SCP. So even though I'm leaving my switch a "shell" as far as ESXi is concerned, I still retain the functionality I may need when I'm in a pinch. So, with Management.2.2 created, we'll assign it the IP address we'll use for SSH, SCP or whatever BSD-like TCP/IP services we wish to use.

Note the inclusion of a default gateway of 192.168.1.1. This is important as it provides the route needed from the 192.168.1.0/24 network over to the 192.168.2.0/24 network. Without this, we wouldn't be able to connect to our Tor proxy installed on the OS X VM assigned the 192.168.2.50 address.

Whew! We're finished with the ESXi configuration and have created our DMZ segment! And now we are finally ready to deploy VM instances in the DMZ!!

If you feel like you are going to miss out on the Tor Proxy configuration, fear not. If you don't feel like going through the hassle or don't have any need for a DMZ, you can still follow these instructions from here on out to configure a Tor proxy even if you keep it on your internal network. I wouldn't leave you out in the cold like that!

Continuing with the presumption you've got your OS X installation for the Tor Proxy configured with the default Tor installation in place, we'll go through the following steps to provide the proxy functionality we've been working towards.

Remember, in this model we are only installing the Tor client on the OS X box we want to use as the proxy – there is no need to install Tor on all your clients. It's actually quite simple from here. Launch Tor, and select Settings and then the Advanced icon.

```
# This file was generated by Tor; if you edit it, comments will not be preserved
# The old torrc file was renamed to torrc.orig.1 or similar, and Tor will ignore it

ContactInfo tor at hammerofgod dot com
ControlPort 9051
DataDirectory /Users/thor/.tor
DirPort 9030
DirReqStatistics 0
ExitPolicy reject *:*
HashedControlPassword 16:382D366E6E02F15160D172691B67F12D34AFCD3E04BEFF8A62BBE73DBF
Log notice stdout
Nickname HammerofGod
ORPort 9001
RelayBandwidthBurst 10485760
RelayBandwidthRate 5242880
SocksListenAddress 192.168.2.50
SocksPort 9050
```

This is the default configuration with the Control Port being set at port 9151 on IP 127.0.0.1 (the loopback). Note the "Control Port" is not the same as the port we need to set as the "proxy port" in our browser profile. More specifically, this is called the "SocksPort" and has a default value of 9050. You don't see options for the Socks Port in the dialog box, but you will if you select the Edit Current torrc button. Note, your configuration will look different insofar as the paths to the configuration file and data directory are different, which is based on your installation. The full default configuration is found in the torrc file which looks like this:

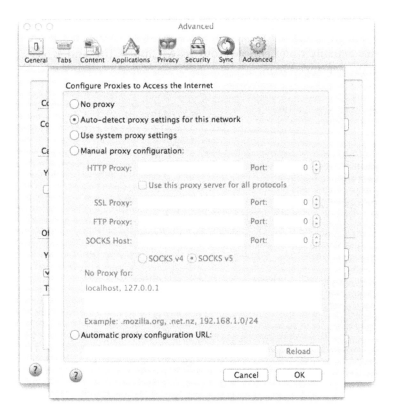

You may not have all the elements shown, but the ones you will have should be at least:

```
ControlPort 9051
DataDirectory [Your data directory]
DirReqStatistics 0
HashedControlPassword [Your Password Hash]
Log notice stdout
SocksPort 9050
```

We will leave the ControlPort and SocksPort values alone, but we do need to add a new value called SocksListenAddress.

You'll see additional configuration options and values in my configuration which may or may not be present in your configuration file, again, based on which type (if any) actual Tor relay-type options you've selected. The important key/value pair for our purposes is the line:

```
SocksListenAddress 192.168.2.50
```

If you followed the previous ESXi configuration instructions to the letter, your OS X Tor Proxy IP will be 192.168.2.50. If not, then you will replace this value with the IP address of your OS X's TCP/IP network address. Without the addition of this key/value, which you will have to type in yourself in the torrc editor window, the default listen port will be 127.0.0.1 even though you don't actually see it explicitly specified.

Save this configuration, exit Tor and relaunch Tor (just to be sure your changes are applied). If Tor doesn't automatically bring up the Start Tor process, just click Start Tor yourself. And we're done as far as the server proxy service is concerned!

All we have to do now is change the SOCKS port we want to proxy connections to in Firefox (or whatever browser you wish). This is where multiple profiles will make your life much simpler. I have a specific profile on my client explicitly configured to use my OS X Tor Proxy. That way I just select my Tor profile in Firefox when I want my connections to be secure without having to muck about with changing configurations and such.

Launching Firefox with a new profile or an existing profile you wish to use, navigate to your Firefox properties, select the Advanced icon, then select the Network tab, and finally click the Settings button under the Connection heading next to the "Configure how Firefox connects to the Internet" text. The default dialog is as follows:

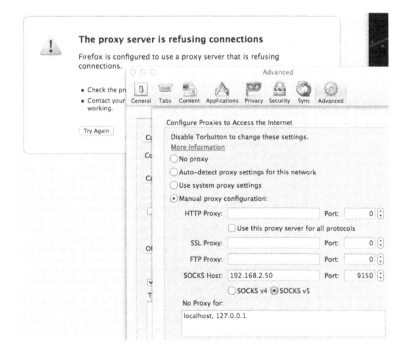

These default settings basically mean that Firefox will automatically detect if you have a proxy server on your network, and if not, to just directly connect to the Internet via your current TCP/IP configuration settings. For our Tor profile, we want to select a Manual proxy configuration and set our SOCKS Host to 192.168.2.50 on port 9050. In this way, when we launch this profile, Firefox will automatically route all outbound SOCKS traffic to our DMZ OS X system. The way your internal address in the 192.168.1.0/24 network will be able to reach the DMZ segment of 192.168.2.0/24 is by way of the default gateway we set for the IP of our Management2.2 vKernel group on vSwitch2.2.

The reason we are selecting the SOCKS protocol (which stands for Sockets Secure) as opposed to what you may normally be familiar with as a HTTP Proxy is because the Tor proxy does not accept actual HTTP Proxy requests – it accepts TCP/IP requests. What this really means for you is that you can actually configure other protocols and applications to use Tor such as mail, remote protocols such as ARD, RDP, SSH, Telnet, etc. or any other IP-based applications. SOCKS also supports UDP forwarding as well if you wish for DNS lookups or the like to also have the source protected by the Tor network! That's way cool, and it's a simple change.

So, to recap our Advanced section, we've learned how to set up an ESXi virtual machine host, configure vSwitches and port groups to create a DMZ segment, populate that DMZ segment with an OS X virtual machine, and configure that VM to act as a proxy for Tor SOCKS connections out to the internet. Finally, we leveraged custom proxy settings in Firefox to make the process of allowing clients on your LAN to easily protect their privacy. I think we've all earned a few hours off to play God of War!

CHAPTER 2

OS Xodus – Media

One of the many superior services OS X offers over Windows is the way it shares and delivers media content.

Back when I was firmly locked into my "Microsoft" mindset, I was more than willing to accommodate the kludge typically required to accomplish any particular goal, and utilizing the Media Center functionality was no exception.

When I began using Media Center, the basic concept was to have a single "server" running as the Media Center role, with external units or systems called "Media Center Extenders" present in order to play media content. This could be a PC, XBox, or by way of specialized equipment such as the Linksys Media Center Extender (WMCE54AG) I purchased at one point. The basic gist was to have a single server to store and deliver content to the extender, which would ultimately be connected to your TV/display and stereo receiver.

The only problem was that it really didn't work well, at all. There were all manner of issues simply getting the Extender to "register" with the Media Center service and the overall content delivery was unreliable and connection issues abounded. Confusing things, to stream media on a Windows machine, "Advanced Media Streaming" configuration options were required to be set globally on the base OS, which further depended on one properly configuring TCP/IP-base sharing options, or you could do it via Media Center. And there was yet another way to share music via Windows Media Player, and so on, and so on.

Remotely controlling media services from mobile devices was, at the time, only available by buying third-party applications. And though I have actually had some some good experiences with writing applications for Windows Phone, the choice of applications that actually worked was almost nil.

But, of course, I ignored all that, kept dredging through the issues, and stuck with Microsoft. Consequently, even after I got things working as well as possible (which was still inferior), I mostly forsook media-sharing in lieu of just watching local content, on the local system.

CONTENTS

Step #1: Basic Media Sharing via iTunes....... 58

Step #2: Advanced Media Control.............. 67
AirPlay................................67

With OS X, all of that disappears.

In this chapter, we'll map out an entire OS X-based Media-sharing environment, taking advantage of the full range of Apple products: Mac OS X, iPhone, iPad, and the Apple TV.

When we're finished, we'll have a seriously cool, multimedia setup, as illustrated in Diagram 2.1; but we'll have to take it in steps.

Regarding Apple TV, you should know it doesn't only act as a "client" for viewing media content, but the Apple TV itself acts as a "server" of sorts, in that it can have media content redirected *to* it *from* your other Apple devices. We'll go into more detail, of course, but for now, let's review Diagram 2.1 so as to get an idea of how our end-result system works.

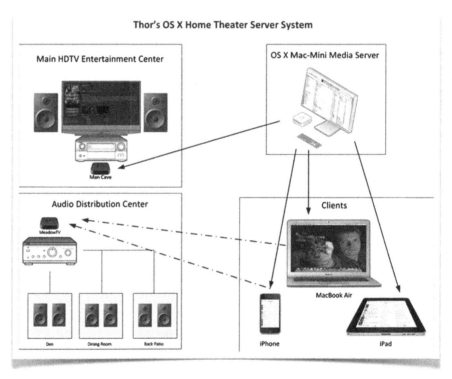

DIAGRAM 2.1

This is actually the system I have at home. The solid arrows indicate a client pulling down media from the server, indicating the direction of the media delivery. The dash-dot-dash lines indicate a client "redirecting" media to the Apple TVs, as described below. I've split the diagram into four main objects:

1. The "Main HDTV Entertainment Center" big screen TV and amp where I do my "sit down" movie watching and game playing.
2. What I call the "Audio Distribution Center," which I'll explain more about later. Even though it is purely an audio application, I've got another Apple TV named "MeadowTV" connected to this receiver.
3. My "OS X Mac-Mini Media Server" running OS X Mavericks and iTunes. It's got all my music, movies, TV shows, pictures, etc. stored there, and I'm sharing various playlists and media objects out to my client devices.
4. The "Clients": These consist of a couple of other Macs, a PC (not really, as I don't have any PCs anymore, but you very well may), a couple of iPads, and a couple of iPhones. The Apple TVs are actually "clients" as well, but let's keep those as part of the main system and the audio center.

The main entertainment center consists of an HDTV, a receiver/amp/video switch unit, speakers, and an Apple TV aptly named "Man Cave." This is also where my PS3 is connected. The Apple TV is used to play content on the HTDV directly from the iTunes Store, Netflix (by way of the Netflix app installed on the Apple TV), and of course the OS X Media Server's shared content. The Apple TV can also stream content directly from iCloud, and new functionality is being added all the time.

The "Audio Distribution Center" is simply a stereo amplifier with outputs to an eight-port speaker switching device from which the speaker wires are run to other rooms in the house. These consist of the upstairs den, the dining room area, and outdoor speakers on the back patio. The reason I have the Apple TV connected is not to act as a client to play media *from* my server, but rather to act as a redirector to play music *to* as I just mentioned. The Apple TV supports a function called AirPlay, allowing you to take the audio and video output from your OS X Mac, iPad, or iPhone and redirect it to the Apple TV itself.

As it relates to the Apple TV connected to the main HDTV ("Man Cave"), this allows me to play audio and video sources from my iPad on the HDTV itself by way of the Apple TV unit. Examples would be, say, a YouTube video or something I want my wife or little boy to see. But as it relates to the Audio Distribution Center, it allows me to simply redirect the audio output from the music on my iPhone, to play anywhere in the house that I want it to.

By way of example: As would be typical, in addition to music shared from the Server, I've got my own *locally* stored songs on my iPhone synchronized from the iTunes server. To be specific, I synchronize music to my iPhone by plugging it into the server and using iTunes to synchronize playlists, application, ringtone, etc. This can also be done via WiFi, but I physically plug mine in. This is how I keep music on the iPhone/iPad itself so as to play "local" music stored there as I go about my day.

However, with the Apple TV configured the way it is, if I'm out in the backyard pushing my son in the swing, I can simply choose the output device from my phone to be the Apple TV connected to the audio receiver (MeadowTV) and ask Siri to play a song. By default, the iPhone plays music directly on the phone itself either out of the speaker or via the headphone jack. But if I select MeadowTV as my output device via AirPlay, it will then immediately begin playing out of the speakers on the back patio by way of the amp connected to the Apple TV. I can, of course, pause, switch songs, and even alter the volume directly from my phone. This obviously requires my iPhone to be connected to my home WiFi, and as such, I can play the music I want from my OS X iTunes server as well, but still redirect it to MeadowTV.

We'll discuss more on how to do this in a bit, but let's first get the general Media Sharing stuff handled for our first step.

STEP #1: BASIC MEDIA SHARING VIA iTUNES

iTunes allows for the sharing of media by way of a feature called "Home Sharing." With OS X, the ability to securely connect clients to share files, media, printers, and other content is automatically available by way of the Bonjour networking service. To use home sharing, simply turn on Home Sharing under the iTunes Edit -> Home Sharing menu item. You'll need an Apple ID to turn it on, but you simply sign in and you're ready to share your media.

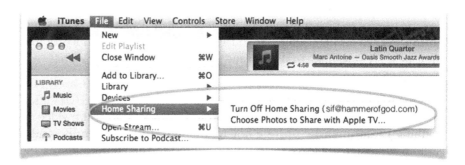

For clients to connect, you also turn on Home Sharing on them and shared media automatically shows up based on what you've decided to share.

I've spoken with many folks using Windows who've had a difficult time setting up media sharing, as they don't know whether to go into Advanced Network Settings to turn on Media Streaming, File Sharing, and Network Discovery or whether to go into HomeGroup and use that. I've also spoken with folks who've purchased a couple of Windows 7 Home systems only to find out that you can't use HomeGroup with Windows 7 Home. Nor, of course, can you use Media Center. Go figure. Windows 7 ships in what MSFT calls "editions." Another word for it is "cripple-ware." If you purchased Windows 7 Home, you can't use HomeGroups, Media Center, and a vast number of other services. You'll have to pay to upgrade to Windows Home Premium, Professional, Ultimate, or Enterprise editions, each with a different cost; and each with different levels of handicap. And, of course, each of these comes with a different level of trying to figure out how to get things to work (or not to work, as the case may be).

With OS X, you get everything when you buy your Mac. No "in place upgrades," no crippled software, and no convoluted "10 ways of not doing something" options to wade through.

So let's get started:

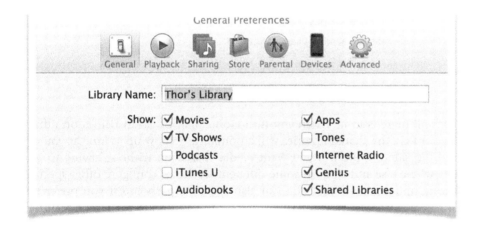

Once Home Sharing has been turned on, you have to select what Media you're going to share. This is done within iTunes under Preferences -> Sharing Tab. First, you'll see the General Tab, where you specify the name of your Library.

In the Sharing Tab I'm just going to go ahead and share all media. On that note, my "main rig" where I keep copies of my local music has over 25,000 songs on it. If you have a monstrous amount of media, then you might want to break it up into Playlists, and share those Playlists rather than just sharing all media. It will make your clients far more responsive when searching through media; 25,000 songs is a lot to push out over the network each time a client goes looking for a tune.

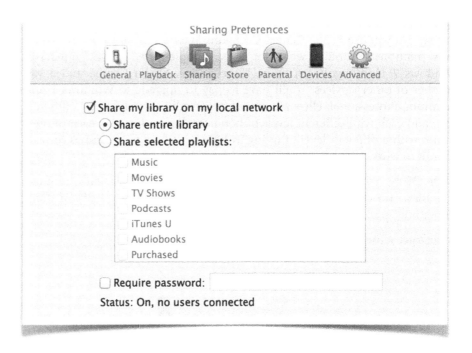

That's all there is to it. When you turn Home Sharing on in iTunes on other Macs or PCs, the shared libraries will automatically show up as long as you've used the same Apple IDs you want media shared on without having to go somewhere else and turn on some different service or configure other special sharing options. Note that you can also specify a password if you prefer to further secure access to your iTunes sharing in addition to the Home Sharing requirement.

Of course from your iPhone, iPad or other iDevice, the configuration is a little bit different. You'll need to go into the Settings utility, and select the media application (Music, Video, etc.) you want to have connected to a shared OS X resource, and turn on Home Sharing there. This is what you'll see on your iPhone.

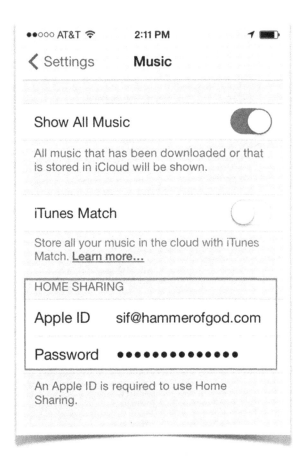

Turning on Home Sharing on the iPad looks just a bit different:

Now that Home Sharing is turned on for your iDevices, you simply open your Music application, select More from the bottom, and then Shared listed as the last "More" item.

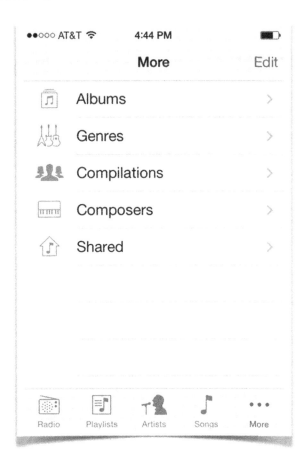

If you don't see the Shared menu list item, then you've not properly set up Home Sharing on your device, or you've used a different Apple ID.

When you select Shared, you'll see all the Libraries you're sharing on your network:

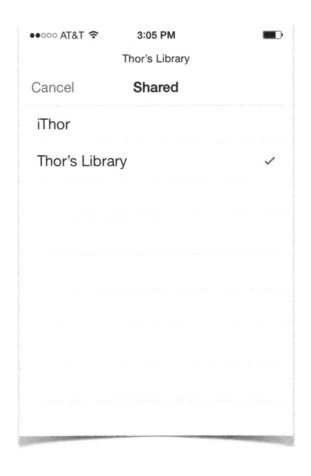

Once you select the Library you wish to use, you'll then be presented with the items shared within that Library:

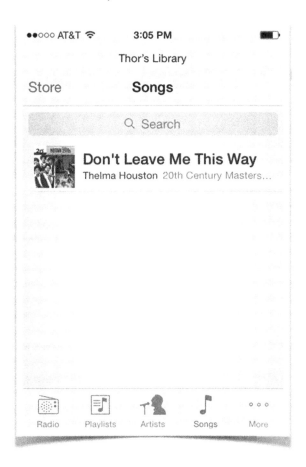

In the previous example, I just shared one song I downloaded so as not to clutter up my screenshot on the iPhone. The following iPad screenshot shows the more typical shared media. list:

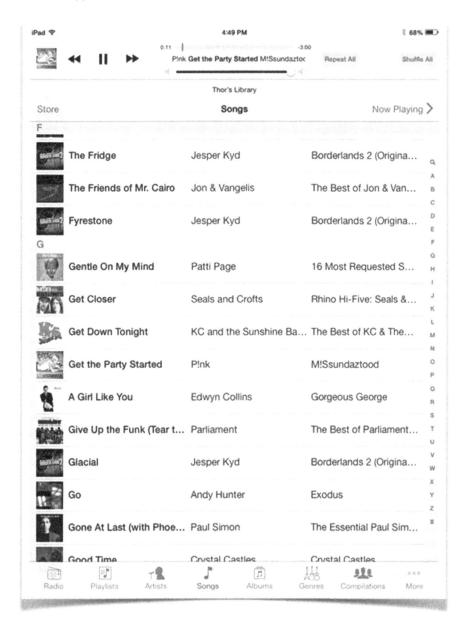

And that is literally all there is to it. I don't think a bunch of screenshots are necessary for other media types, but if you want to watch shared video from your Libraries then you'll go into Settings on your iDevices, scroll down to Video, and turn Home Sharing on in the same way. This "media-type-by-media-type" access to shared resources configuration is only on mobile iDevices. From another iTunes client, you'll see all media types shared.

STEP #2: ADVANCED MEDIA CONTROL

Now, let's get into some of the more fun stuff. In the previous scenario, we simply specified what media we wished to share out to other devices, from whatever Macs we shared our libraries on.

Next, we are going to get into configuring the actual delivery of media from one device to another. Let me clarify that distinction: When I say things like "server" and "client," what I mean is the client retrieves content from the server that is sharing out media.

When I say "delivery" of media, I mean the actual device you are using will "redirect" audio and video content to be seen and heard on another device – in this case, as described in the initial example, the Apple TV via AirPlay.

AirPlay

When I found out about AirPlay I was pretty excited. Knowing I could be on my iPhone looking at something and that I could immediately present the content on my 55″ HDTV was quite cool.

But setting it up was actually more difficult than I thought. Let me clarify that by way of a *Confession of a previous Microsoft Engineer*. When I found out about AirPlay, I went to the Apple TV to look for some place where I could download the drivers to support AirPlay functionality. I found nothing. I got on the Internet, again looking for whatever App I had to download, and how to configure this newfound functionality. I found nothing. Even with what I consider substantial Google-Fu skilz, I couldn't find the App or the drivers.

That's because there aren't any. They are already there. Much to my embarrassment I finally came upon a simple one-paragraph explanation telling me to simply select the Apple TV I wanted to use from the iPhone or the iPad.

You see, being an ex-Microsoft guy, I naturally assumed I had to install client and server components to use AirPlay. But I didn't. When I turned on Home Sharing on the Apple TV, it automatically shows up as an output device on my clients without me having to do a single thing. Duh.

Incredulous, sitting there in front of the HDTV, I simply swiped up and lo and behold, there right in front of me was the option for AirPlay:

In my defense, I swear I'd done that before as I was out sitting somewhere looking for configuration options. The thing was, if there wasn't an Apple TV on the same Home Sharing network, iOS didn't show me the option. How dare they?? How dare Apple not show me an option for something I couldn't do!! I'm kidding, obviously. But that said, had this been a Microsoft implementation, they would show the option for what you couldn't do and you would find out you couldn't do it only after trying to. There's actually some logic there, and I would be less than honest if I said I wouldn't have done it that way as well (the Microsoft way). But as you get more and more used to working with OS X, and iOS, you'll realize the level of intuitiveness actually serves you: if you can't do something, then don't give someone the option. This is particularly true in interfaces with limited screen size.

Regardless of one's position on that manner of logic, that's how it works with iOS.

So I touched AirPlay, and there was Man Cave.

Of course, I say "no *%&^$ way," touch Man Cave, go back to my Coldplay song, touch "play" and immediately out of my speakers plays "Warning Sign."

It was that simple, and the functionality was already there, ready to be used without me having to install any apps, drivers, or most importantly, go through any additional configuration options. Using Microsoft products had *taught* me to expect unnecessary complexity to the point that I, quite literally, missed what was right in front of my eyes.

Before I get into AirPlay video, let's apply what we just did to the overall configuration laid out in the beginning of the chapter. My "Audio Distribution Center" as discussed is simply a stereo amp with my Apple TV's optical audio output going to one of the amp's optical inputs. In my case, I bought a separate Apple TV specifically for this purpose named "Meadow TV." And again as mentioned, I've got an eight-port audio switch with speaker runs made throughout the house. The beautiful thing about this is that I can just leave that amp on set to whatever volume I'm comfortable with, and whenever I wanted, I could just redirect my music output from my iPhone or iPad to Meadow TV. What is really cool is that the Apple TVs audio volume is also controlled by the iPhone or iPad. So while the song is playing, if I adjust the volume on my phone, the volume is adjusted from the Apple TV's output. Note that you're not limited to iDevice clients. iTunes automatically detects Apple TVs and allows you to redirect audio as well. In fact, iTunes allows you to redirect audio to multiple Apple TVs simultaneously! This would be an awesome way to distribute music in an office environment without having to run wires everywhere. Or a club, or whatever.

Now, on to video.

After the success with the iPhone, I was excited to try video. So I grab my iPad and go to the App Store, swipe up, and sure enough – there it was:

This time I've selected Man Cave and chosen "Mirroring." This will cause the iPad to send both Audio and Video currently displayed to the Apple TV.

Unfortunately, you can't get a screenshot of the Apple TV itself (unless you jailbreak it) so I've got to show you a photo:

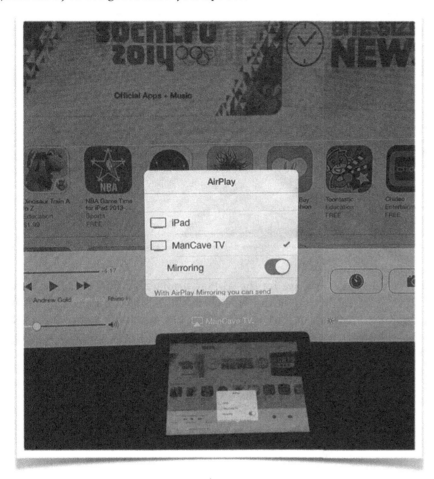

As you can see, everything on the iPad's screen (bottom center) is now being displayed on my HDTV. If I were to put on a video, or browse to the Internet, everything I see on my iPad will be presented to the Man Cave Apple TV. Very cool.

So there we have it. With just a few simple steps, you can transform the way you view and present audio and video in your media services.

Before we end, since we're on the subject of Apple TV, let's see some of the other cool things you can do from your Mac itself – and not just with audio and video from iPads. This example is with my MacBook Pro, but it will work on any OS X client; and as you can see, you can mirror your display in the same way we did with our iDevices.

An OS X client will *automatically* detect the presence of an Apple TV without you having to do a thing. The AirPlay icon will be displayed in your notification bar at the top of your screen:

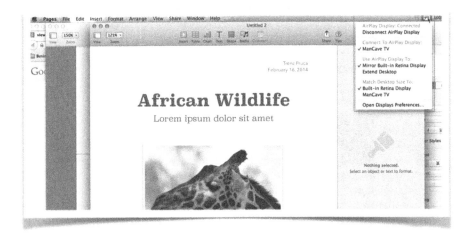

Here I've selected Man Cave for the AirPlay display. But note that now we've got some different options. I can "Match Desktop Size" to that of either my MacBook Pro's display, or have my MacBook Pro match the size of the Apple TV. As with the iPad, this will completely duplicate my MacBook Pro screen on my HDTV, even the Dock.

But here's where things get **really** cool. Not only can you mirror your OS X display, but you can tell OS X to use the Apple TV as an *extra monitor* all by itself. This is done quite simply by selecting "Extend Desktop" instead of "Mirror."

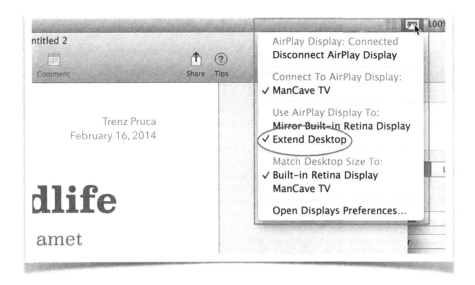

Now we have the option of opening applications on our OS X machine, and literally dragging them over to the Apple TV as if the monitor were directly connected. Here I've got the same Pages doc open, but this time I've opened up Safari and gone to the apple.com site displayed on the Apple TV. I've even pulled up the Dock on the extended Apple TV AirPlay display.

In conclusion, we've seen exactly how easy it is to configure a full range of media sharing and redirecting options in OS X. We've even learned how to create an extended monitor over your wireless network via Apple TV. Not only can many of the features we've discussed not even be implemented on a Windows network (natively), but even if they could, the configuration and use of such a feature-set would be arduous at best.

CHAPTER 3

The Interface

As I was developing this chapter, it became evident it would be the most challenging. Not because of the technical requirements or expertise required to cover the OS X interface, but because of the challenge of identifying what aspects of the interface I would choose to cover. There are so many amazingly cool things about OS X, particularly as regards the initial "discovery" of the operating system, that it became harder and harder for me to isolate the applications and processes I thought you may find most valuable.

However, I had to shake them out, so here we have it. I kind of like the fact this chapter will be more of a "personal" one in that I'm basically going to share a handful of things I found to be the most interesting. And of course there's the degree to which I'm going to compare how much Windows pales in comparison to OS X, which had its own challenges: there are so many… Some may seem trivial at first, but as you actually start using OS X you'll see that the simple things can make a really big difference. So here we go.

MULTIPLE MONITORS AND CUSTOMIZATION

In its simplest terms, the most important aspect of an operating system is the user interface, and that interface is presented to you via the monitor.

Similar to Windows, OS X allows you to use multiple monitors and to customize the virtual location of those monitors. I highly recommend that you go out and buy yourself additional monitors for your OS X box. You'll be glad you did.

CONTENTS

Multiple Monitors and Customization 75

Finder and Navigation 78

Quick Look 85

Tags 86

Tagging With Spotlight 88

Apple Defaults and Script Editor 93

Encrypted Disk Images 99

Intelligent, Multi-Choice Dialog Boxes 108

Intelligent Shared File System Updates 110

Intelligent File Copy .. 116

Consider the following Arrangement dialog image from the "Displays" applet in System Preferences:

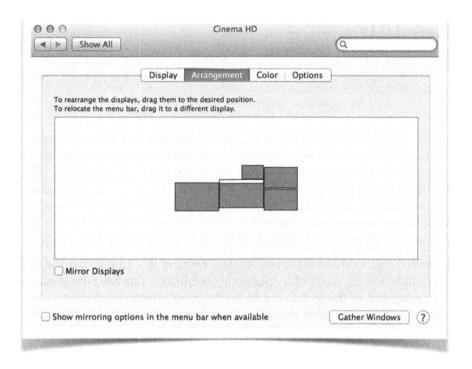

In my case, I've got five monitors connected to my main OS X rig: Two 30″ HD Cinema Displays, two 23″ HD Cinema Displays, and a USB pico projector that I use to project performance graphs on my wall. My two 30″ displays (the center being my main display) are next to each other with the second on the left, and my two 23″ displays are stacked on top of each other to the right. The pico projector is actually mounted to the wall behind me and projects upon the white-space of my wall centered between the main monitor and the two stacked monitors.

However, you'll see that I have the virtual representation of the projector monitor sitting directly on top of my main 30″ display. The image object of the projector is actually touching the top of my main monitor, and this is an important placement feature as it tells OS X that if I move my mouse from either touching monitor, the cursor will immediately and *seamlessly* move into that monitor space.

However, unlike Windows, OS X allows you to take advantage of a very simple yet powerful positioning feature. Consider the following image, now updated:

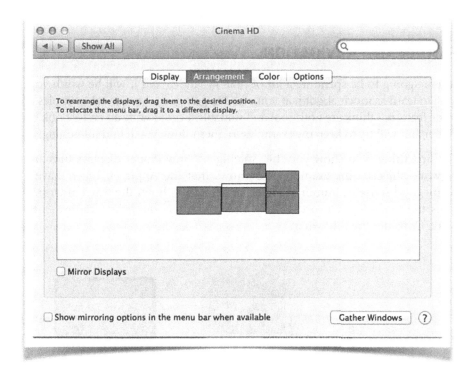

You'll notice now I've moved the icon for my projector up above my monitor just a bit; it is no longer positioned to "touch" the main monitor. On a Windows machine, this does not change the behavior of moving the mouse about from screen to screen; however, in OS X, moving the monitors "apart" from one another causes the mouse cursor to be "sticky" on adjacent monitors.

With five monitors it can sometimes be a bit tricky to keep track of where my cursor is, particularly when you fly around different applications as I do. When my mouse pointer goes up "above" the actual main monitors and into the projector image, it's hard for me to see it, as my particular projector is tiny and doesn't allow for exact focus at the 8-foot distance. And it's not exactly the brightest thing in the world. The main point here is that I really have no need to move my mouse up to my projector monitor, as my applications are specifically positioned and OS X always puts them back exactly where I left them.

So, moving the virtual monitor arrangement away from the other monitors "holds" the mouse on the main monitor, unless I actually "push" it up to the projector screen. This keeps my mouse from accidentally getting lost up there. I can still move it up to the projector, but I have to confirm my intention by telling OS X that I really want to go there.

FINDER AND NAVIGATION

You are going to be spending a lot of time in Finder, and it will be worth your time to learn as much about it as you can. I'm going to cover several examples of some features I think are both cool and valuable. I could write an entire book on Finder, but will try to keep my examples to ones I think you'll find interesting.

The first thing is to show you the "intelligent" way Finder displays files and network objects. This example also shows that the Apple engineers have a pretty good sense of humor as well. This example shows the way Finder presents the icons for network objects and computers on your local area network. Consider the following:

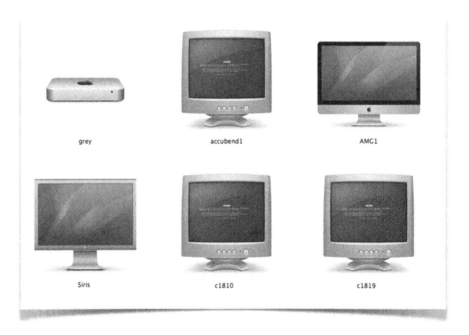

Finder doesn't just show default, built-in icons for Mac systems as does Windows – it actually determines what type of computer is on your network and displays the appropriate icons. You'll see "grey" is the Mac Mini you've probably by now become familiar with. The interesting thing here is that grey shows up in the list of other network objects even though it is a Back to My Mac system located at my house. This seamless integration of objects with the other systems on my office LAN in itself shows how Apple makes navigation between objects simple and easy. You'll notice further that AMG is an iMac and Siris (It's spelled like that on purpose) is a desktop Mac. Of course, Windows machines must be represented by generic icons because, to be blunt, Windows doesn't really know what it's running on and there's no mechanism by which one can query the system to find out. This is yet another example of where one must purchase third-party utilities to do something OS X does out of the box. What I thought was awesome is that the Windows computer icons are all showing the "blue screen" display. I about busted a gut laughing when I first saw that, and thought it was a wonderful jab on Apple's part.

There are several Finder "view" options available to you, each with its own set of benefits and options. The previous screenshot of the network objects had them viewed as "Icons," which show either object-based icons, or in the case of files, thumbnail views of files or images.

Before we get into the other views, there are a couple of options within the Finder preferences I want to identify, as my screenshots are representative of these options being selected.

In Finder -> Preferences you'll find generalized options such as what items to include on the desktop, what to show in the sidebar, and "Tag" options (which I'll discuss in a bit), but the options I'm interested in are in the Advanced tab:

This is totally up to you, but I've always selected to "Show all filename extensions." Even though there is a specific "Type" column that indicates what manner of file is being displayed, I just like seeing the entire filename in the Name column. This is why you'll see filename extensions in my screenshots. I also choose to have the Current Folder be the default for Finder-based searches (as opposed to Spotlight, which I will also discuss shortly).

In addition to these Finder Preferences settings, I have selected to show optional bars in my Finder window. While the Tab Bar and Sidebar are shown by default, the Path Bar and Status Bar are not. The Path Bar shows the full path to the folder and file you are currently in while the Status Bar shows what files you've selected and how much space you have on the drive you are on. You can see I have all the options selected (otherwise it wouldn't show me the "Hide" options).

The Path and Status Bars show up on the bottom of the Finder window. By way of example, this screenshot shows you the full path to the folder containing the supporting documents for this book.

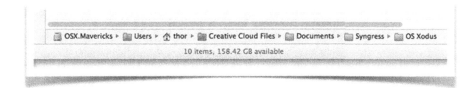

Again, it doesn't matter if you use these settings, but now you'll know why you may see them in screenshots and not in your personal Finder view.

And with that, let's get back to our View definitions.

Following the order in which Finder lists the views, "List View" is the second available view, and can be automatically switched to by using the Command+2 keyboard combination. List view, as the name suggests, gives us a line-by-line list of all files and directories within the current directory. It also gives us "intelligent" column data based on the type of files Finder determines are in the directory.

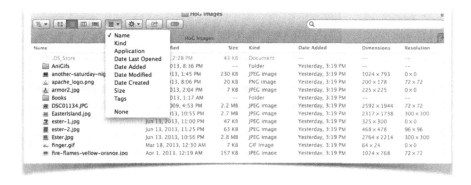

I'll provide a larger image of this directory shortly, but this screenshot is showing my "HoG Images" folder, with the files listed primarily by Name as you can see by the selection in the Sort option. There are two things I want you to notice. One, to the far left we see columns for Dimensions and Resolution. I did not add these columns – Finder automatically added them because it determined the folder contains mostly images. Secondly, notice that the sorting of Name orders the list alphabetically without respect to the item type. Folders and files are listed together in alphabetical order. This is fine because it's what I asked for, but unlike Windows, OS X allows us to specify a secondary grouping sort.

If you hold down the Option key while clicking on the Sort icon, you'll see a similar (but different) set of options.

With my primary sort being Name, I'm going to Option+Click the sort icon and select Type. Now look at how my files are sorted:

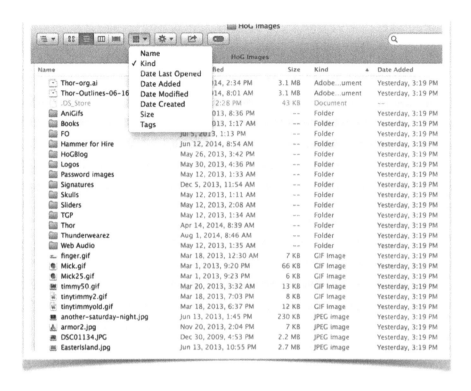

Now we see that our folders and files are still sorted by Name, but they are grouped by Type. All of our GIF images are together sorted by Name as are our folders. This is very cool and offers a lot of flexibility in your views.

I will explain this in more detail later in this chapter, but take a moment to look at this image and locate the ".DS_Store" document. You'll notice it is greyed out in the list; this means the file is "hidden" as it is a system file. In Windows, you can show hidden files, but they are just listed along with the rest of them. Finder makes sure you know the file is hidden by changing the way it displays it for you. I'll show you how to display hidden files in a moment by way of another very powerful tool called Apple Script.

Back to the list, Finder's List view also provides intelligent changes in the way data is displayed based on what actions you take in the view. By way of example, you see in the previous image that the Date field provides full date details in the format of MMM, DD, YYYY, HH:MM. For instance, "Mick.gif" was last modified Mar 1, 2013, 9:20 PM.

While this is great information to have, it's a bit verbose for me, and it takes up too much space in my list view. What's really cool is that if I shorten the column width, Finder will automatically change the date format for me as follows:

Now the date format is simply M/DD/YY. It takes up far less space but still gives me the information I need. It's this type of intuitive, automatic, and "natural" features Apple builds into their interface that makes it superior.

Our next view is "Column View" and it too offers up its own particular benefits. It took me a bit to get used to Column View, but I particularly like its "file preview" features.

Column View shows you a side-by-side view of files in a top-down, left-to-right hierarchy. This shot shows my "temp" folder in the far left column, then its contents (being the "HoG Images" folder) in a second column, and further the HoG Images folder contents in yet another column. If I select the "grin.jpg" file, Finder will then show me a preview of the file in its own column with full file information.

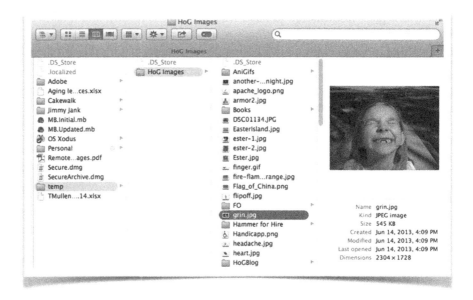

The preview feature works with text files, document files, PDFs, images, or any other file that Finder can identify.

Finally, we have the Cover Flow view. If you use iTunes, you'll be quite familiar with this type of file view. I find Cover Flow to be of particular value when browsing through image folders. Basically, Cover Flow provides the detail of List View with a multi-file preview option at the top.

With Cover Flow I not only see the selected image preview, but I can see several of the adjacent files in the folder as well. You'll notice the scroll bar under the "grin.jpg" footer of the Cover Flow preview – this allows me to very quickly scroll through all the images so I can visually identify what file I want.

And this is what we do with images. When I port over images from my camera and I end up with 30 images named something like "IMG001-22.jpg" there's no way I'm going to know what file I'm looking for by name. Cover Flow allows me to visually scan the directory to easily find the file I'm looking for.

QUICK LOOK

Column and Cover Flow views are not the only way to get a preview of files. There is a very cool Finder feature called "Quick Look" that also gives you a preview of a file.

To use Quick Look, simply hit the space bar with a file selected and you'll get a separate pop-up window previewing the file:

The best thing I like about Quick Look is that I can simply use my arrow keys to move up or down through my directory to automatically Quick Look at the other files without ever leaving the Quick Look window.

The flexibility Finder gives us in regard to the way we sort, view, preview, or edit files is outstanding. The fact that we have so many options and preferences again shows how Apple designs their operating systems to provide the user with options they want and need, and not options they dictate the user must use.

TAGS

Finder also allows us to organize files and folders in a very interesting way using what are called "Tags." Tags are actually color-based file attributes that can be used to organize and view files and folders irrespective of their representative location on your drives. By default, Tag names are the colors which they represent, but you can change the Tag name to whatever you want and add new tags. If there are specific files that are in different locations, but there is some criteria by which I choose to group them in a logical list view, I simply select the file, click on my Tabs icon, and tag the file with whichever Tag I choose.

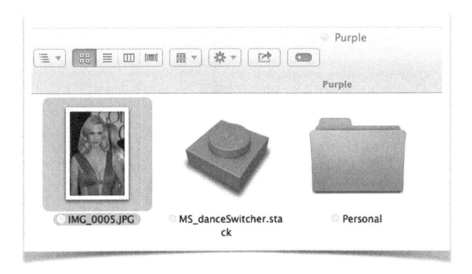

Here I've gone through and Tagged some files associated with a particular web project I'm developing. I've got an image of January Jones, a Rapid Weaver stack, and a folder named "Personal."

These files and folder are all in different places, and even spread over different drives in my system. However, if I want to view them, all I have to do is (in this case) select my "Purple" tag and these files are immediately displayed.

What's great about Tags is that you can assign multiple tags to a single file. For instance, January Jones is both tagged as Purple for this particular web project and Red for my desktop images that cycle through my various monitors. Red is for "hot" in this case.

I also have another use for Tags, and that's to sort of track my "progress" as I edit or take any particular action on a number of files.

In my "real" life, I write a lot of code and architect enterprise database models. There is a lot of data moving about, and some in the form of external files received from vendors and financial institutions. Inevitably, these files come in the form of date-based filenames such as FIN091214.DAT or the like. Many times there are dozens in a directory, and in some cases I want to go through those files to check for data formats. When using Windows, the only really effective way of "marking off" the files as I checked them was to literally write it down on a piece of paper. I searched around and found this suggestion from a Microsoft employee in the Windows 7 forum:

> There is no option to know if the files are read on Windows Explorer on the computer. Flags are only available in Outlook and are not available in Windows Explorer.
> As a workaround you may enable the Date accessed in Windows Explorer.
> 1.   Open **Windows Explorer** and right click on **empty space**.
> 2.   Click on **Sort By** and click on **More**.
> 3.   Scroll down the list to find **Date Accessed** and put a **tick mark**.
> 4.   Click **OK**.
> Now check if that works.
> However you may use your favorite search engine and check if there are any non Microsoft tools available as such to signify only the "read" files.
> **NOTE**: Using Third Party Software, including hardware drivers can cause serious problems that may prevent your computer from booting properly. Microsoft cannot guarantee that any problems resulting from the use of Third Party Software can be solved. Using Third Party Software is at your own risk.

That is obviously a horrible solution, and it didn't even work for what I was doing. Now that I'm an OS X convert, it is trivial for me to simply mark off the files I've edited with a tag. In fact, I use multiple tags to signify if I've determined some data is problematic, or if I need to just go back and make sure.

In this example, I've got a list of files I need to go through and check that the bank sent me. And no, I didn't ask them to name them "Thor," they did that on their own. When I've examined a file and it's OK, I mark it with a Green tag. If I've reviewed it and determined there is a problem I mark it Green as read, and then Red as problematic. If I need to go back and review, I mark it Green as read and Yellow as a potential problem. I could certainly mark problems just with Red and reviews as Yellow, but I want to be able to see everything I've reviewed along with the problems. In this way, I can pull up Green tags and see everything I need!

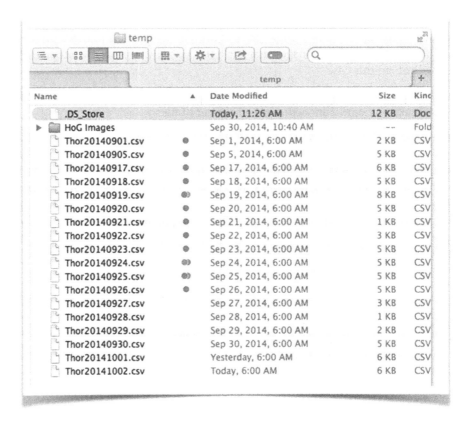

I edit these files in a Temp folder, but as you can see I've edited most of them and only a couple need review and only one has a problem.

TAGGING WITH SPOTLIGHT

When I first started with OS X, I was slow to adopt the color-Tagging because I really didn't have a frame of reference from which to apply the various logical uses for tagging – meaning, I came from Windows and never considered what I could do with such a feature. Since, I've obviously become dependent upon this feature as I use it every day.

However, tagging with color isn't always the best way of going about organizing and, more importantly, *locating* files you may wish to find. This is where Spotlight Tagging comes in.

Spotlight is an amazing system-wide search tool which has been identified by many of the folks I've converted as their most used and favorite feature of OS X. In its simplest form, Spotlight is an interface you can use to find anything you wish on your entire system. Spotlight keeps a constantly updated database index of files, folders, and applications. It also looks within files to allow you to search for specific content in, say, a Pages document. It even indexes content in email, contacts, reminders, notes, and virtually everywhere within the system you may want to find something.

By way of example, I'll invoke Spotlight with Command+Spacebar to pull up the Spotlight "search" bar at the top right of your active screen. You can also click the "Magnifying Glass" icon in the main Menu Bar.

In a previous example of copying files, I used "Oingo Boingo" as an example. But before I show this feature, I'm going to send myself an email about the song "Grey Matter" off the *Skeletons in the Attic* album. While you are obviously reading this offline, the point I'm going to illustrate is that Spotlight's indexing feature is immediate.

Invoking Spotlight, I'm going to type in "Oingo."

"Top Hits" are first based on filenames. The "Oingo.tiff" file is actually the source image file from the screenshot I showed you of the "Replace" dialog box during the file copy.

Spotlight then identified the fact "Oingo" as a textual element is contained within two documents, ironically enough being this Pages chapter file.

Folders were then identified because the name of the parent folder for *Skeletons in the Attic* is "Oingo Boingo."

We then see the mail item I just sent to myself – it immediately showed up after sending the email.

Then of course we have a listing of all Oingo Boingo MP3 files. Clicking on the email item will bring up the email. Clicking on the folder will open a Finder window directly in that folder. And clicking on a song will start it playing in iTunes.

It's a very fast, powerful, and fantastic feature of OS X.

Continuing with our example, there's another feature of Spotlight we're going to use called "Spotlight Comments." In OS X there are a number of attributes that go along with any particular file. One of these attributes is an extension that allows users to enter in whatever manner of text description and/or tags they wish on a file.

The "Oingo.tiff" file referenced is in a particular folder I have where I've organized all the image files used in this book. I'm going to navigate to that folder, highlight Oingo.tiff, and do a COMMAND+i to pull up the Get Info dialog box:

▼ More Info:

    Dimensions: 439 × 180
    Color space: RGB
    Color profile: sRGB IEC61966-2.1
  Alpha channel: Yes
    Last opened: Today, 9:30 AM

▼ Name & Extension:

    Oingo.tiff

⬜ Hide extension

▼ Comments:

    TheHooch

▼ Open with:

  🐢 Preview.app   ⬍

Use this application to open all documents like this one.

  Change All...

In this clipped portion of the Get Info dialog, I see image information, the filename, and a "Comments" window. This "comment" section allows us to enter whatever text we wish, and this text will be indexed along with other Spotlight data.

For illustration, I've entered "TheHooch" in this file as well as in the image file just shown. You may remember that "TheHooch" is the default password used in "Thor's Password Machine," so we'll see where else this phrase may pop up when we now go into Spotlight again and search for "TheHooch."

Interestingly enough, the first document hit was this Pages file I'm working on as I type this. Spotlight was able to index this document even though it was open and I've not closed it since I began writing this section. Amazing.

Under images we now see both Oingo.tiff and OingoComments.tiff; this is of course because we added custom text-element tags to the Comments of the file, which Spotlight immediately indexed. Also, you can see that Spotlight intelligently separates the documents and files it finds not just on the file extension, but for the typical usage context of the file. The file inc.functions.php is a "document" just like a PDF file, yet Spotlight knows that PHP files are a special *class* of document, and groups those files within a "Developer" section of its own.

Spotlight even was able to pull references to TheHooch which were in my server logs as I tested my PHP code on Black (Like My Heart) as evidenced by the "201304xx_xxxxxx.Black (like my heart)" log files.

In addition, if one performs a Command+Click on a file in the Spotlight list, Finder will open a new window taking you directly to the file.

So we see that we have multiple options and logical approaches to tagging, grouping, and retrieving files, folders, and even contents of documents and emails.

There are hundreds of other intuitive and cool things you can do with Finder, and I think you're going to have a great time exploring and learning as you become more and more familiar with your Mac.

APPLE DEFAULTS AND SCRIPT EDITOR

OS X applications can have hundreds of preferences or options that are set by default, yet easily changed by the user when customization of the user interface or application operation is wanted or needed.

In most cases, these options are enabled, disabled, or set to default values by way of the applications' "plist" file. A plist file, which stands for "property list," is an XML-based, human readable file that is parsed by an application upon start (or when changes are made by the user) which loads up a list of properties or preferences which drive particular behaviors, set interface viewing options, or drive any number of features or functions within the application.

As discussed earlier, the listing of my ".DS_Store" file in the HoG Images folder, though a hidden file, was the result of changing the default behavior of Finder, which is to hide hidden folders and files. More on that in a bit.

Windows has a method by which default operating system and application options are set, added, or altered, called the system Registry. The Windows Registry is a massive database presented as a single entity to the user but which is actually made up of many files called "hives." It is probably the worst method I've seen to implement functionality management between applications and the operating system. It is bloated, difficult to use and/or understand, and the improper deletion or alteration of distinct operating system registry entries can result in complete system failure.

Distinct property and preference management via individual application plist files is not only blazingly fast, but it isolates changes to preferences and properties to the application. Further, as individual XML files, they can be easily copied, edited, or backed up on a file-by-file basis. By way of example, I don't use Terminal for my bash interface – I use iTerm. iTerm allows for a plethora of different options to be set like colors, backgrounds, and many different behaviors. These options are stored in a file called com.googlecode.iterm2.plist, located in the user's home Library preferences: ~/Library/Preferences. All of the customized options and profiles are stored in this file.

When I make changes to my profiles on my main rig, I would like those changes to be easily updated on my other machines where I also have iTerm running.

If this were a Windows application, I would most likely be screwed as I would have to manually update the settings on each machine. For example, if I went into Outlook and set a lot of custom options, I couldn't simply copy over a configuration file to my other systems running Outlook and be done with it. I *might* be able to copy registry hives over, but doing so would run the risk of mangling the application.

With OS X, I can simply copy that plist file over to my Preferences folder on the target machines and I'm done. I can even copy and paste the XML data through a SSH session if I want. It's super easy and super flexible. It's also secure, as you'll need to authenticate as an administrator to change the file, even if you are logged in as an administrative user. This doesn't happen for processes running as Administrator in Windows, which is why millions and millions of Windows systems are infected by viruses, trojans, and malware. I don't have AV or anti-malware on any of my Mac systems because I don't need it.

While a user certainly could edit plist files to set values for keys, that's probably not the way you should do it because you could still mess something up. That's why there is an OS X option called "defaults" which allows you to set any number of preferences for any number of applications.

Let's take Apple Mail – as you can imagine, there are a huge number of settings, preferences, behaviors, and options you can enable, disable, change, or alter as you please. These are all stored in the com.apple.mail.plist file.

By default, Apple Mail will show "previews" of attached files. Meaning if I drop a PDF file into an email, it will display the contents of that PDF file in the body of the email. This is actually pretty cool because if you are dropping in a lot of files (say, pictures) you can easily see which files are already there as opposed to just filenames.

However, this can also be a bit irritating when you are dropping in a lot of files and you have to move around a bit to get where you are going. As a case in point, one day I was sending my attorney a substantial number of PDF files, and the preview option was getting in my way. One or two is fine, but 20 was not.

Of course, Apple Mail has an option to disable this feature called, you guessed it, "DisableInlineAttachmentViewing." Using this as an example, I'll show you how to use the "defaults" directive. From a bash prompt, simply type in:

```
defaults write com.apple.mail DisableInlineAttachmentViewing -bool
yes
```

The syntax here is the "defaults" directive followed by the action of either read, write, or delete, the plist file identifier, the key you wish to take the action on, and any parameters that go along with the action. In this case we're telling OS X to find the com.apple.mail plist file for us, no matter where it is, and add the bool (which means true or false) to write the value of "yes" (true) to that key.

And this is why using the "defaults" directive is best: earlier you saw that my iTerm plist file was in ~/Library/Preferences. Well, since Apple Mail isn't a third-party app, the com.apple.mail.plist file is located in ~/Library/Containers/com.apple.mail/Data/Library/Preferences folder. You shouldn't be expected to go hunting for the exact location of where the file is (like you would in the Registry), so OS X does the heavy lifting for you.

Upon execution, if you examined the com.apple.mail.plist file, you would see the following entry added to the existing properties in XML format:

```
<key>DisableInlineAttachmentViewing</key>
<true/>
```

This property value will now cause Mail to show attachments and icons and not a preview of the document itself.

Once I was done sending the docs, I simply executed the directive again, this time setting the key to "no" or "false":

```
defaults write com.apple.mail DisableInlineAttachmentViewing
-bool no
```

What is absolutely fantastic about this is that I didn't even have to restart the Mail application for this to take effect. Immediately upon dropping in a file (or selecting a signature with an image) the preview was presented.

This, however, isn't always the case. Returning to our "showing hidden files" option, this too was accomplished by way of using the "defaults" directive with this syntax:

```
defaults write com.apple.finder AppleShowAllFiles -boolean true
```

Setting it to "false" turns off the inclusion of hidden files. For what I assume are performance purposes, Finder only parses its plist options on launch, so you have to restart Finder for the change to take place. That's simple enough: You go to the Apple icon in the top left, select Force Quit, and upon selecting Finder click "Relaunch." But there's an even easier way: In a bash shell, just type "killall Finder" and it will immediately relaunch. Don't worry, you won't lose anything; Finder just restarts and refreshes its property settings.

However, you very well may wish to only show hidden files when you want to, and not all the time. I kind of like it, but I will say that the .DS_Store file will be in every folder, and when you "select all" to copy files, it too will be included if it is not hidden. But you certainly wouldn't want to have to go through that every time you want to turn files on or off.

So let's discuss a way that we can easily turn hidden files on or off, and do so without having to drop into a bash shell each time.

Enter in "AppleScript Editor." The script editor is an extremely powerful built-in utility that allows you to write from the simplest to the most complex script files that can do basically anything you can think of. Of course, the more complex the task, the more you'll need to learn, but it is a great way to automate processes and a fun way to learn how to code, if that's something you're into.

So what we're going to do is write up a quick script that will first read the value of AppleShowAllFiles, and depending on what that value is, turn it on or off. That way we can just run the script and it will toggle back and forth for us. If it's on, the script will turn it off. If it's off, the script will turn it on. After that setting is updated, the script will restart Finder for us. This is what the script looks like:

```
set current_value to do shell script "defaults read com.apple.
finder AppleShowAllFiles"

if current_value = "0" then
        do shell script "defaults write com.apple.finder
AppleShowAllFiles -boolean true"
else
        do shell script "defaults write com.apple.finder
AppleShowAllFiles -boolean false"
end if
do shell script "killall Finder"
```

It's actually quite simple, but provides needed functionality. Here's what it looks like if pasted into the AppleScript Editor itself:

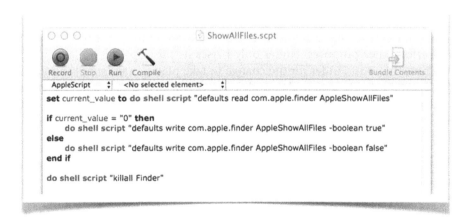

When I click the Run icon, Script Editor will execute the code for me and toggle the setting back and forth for me.

In this example, though, the script file itself had to be opened first. In this case I had ShowAllFiles.scpt on my desktop, so I could just double-click it and hit run and then close it.

But there's a simpler way of doing this, and it is something worth looking at if you have many scripts.

First, though, let's talk about the "Record" button. Record is a great tool that lets you simply go through and perform your tasks while Script Editor analyzes the steps you've taken and converts those actions into AppleScript for you.

Let's say that I like to open up my com.apple.mail.plist file a lot just to look at my preferences. Not necessarily the most realistic example, but a good one as it relates to recording actions in Script Editor.

In a new Script Editor window, I'm going to click record. Then I'm going to open up an application I use called "BBEdit," and then use a feature specific to BBEdit called "Open File By Name." This isn't a standard "Open" function – it's only in BBEdit, a third-party program. I'll put in the full path to my com. apple.mail.plist file, and tell it to open the file.

As I do this, the Script Editor begins populating the window with the script equivalent of the actions I've taken. Once the file is open, I'll click Stop and Script Editor will end the record session. This is what has happened in Script Editor (note this screenshot shows the script after I saved it on my desktop as BBEditMail.scpt):

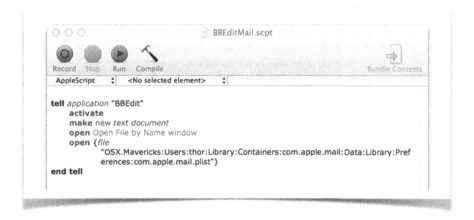

Script Editor did all the hard work for me. The cool thing is that it figured out the menu item name specific to BBEdit and passed that variable through to the "open" script command. It then put the full path to the file, and opened it. Very cool.

Again, all I have to do is double click the BBEditMail.scpt file and hit Run and the Script Editor does it for me. But as you are probably thinking, that's still a few steps too many to go through.

So let's put our scripts at our fingertips for easy access by putting Script Editor functionality right into our main menu bar! With the AppleScript Editor application open, go to preferences and select "Show Script menu in menu bar."

Once you do this, you'll see the AppleScript Editor icon appear up in your menu bar with your other menu bar applications:

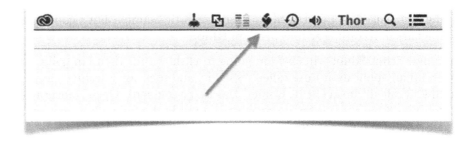

Clicking on this gives us access to AppleScript Editor "Quick Menu" items:

Good enough. What we want to do now is to automatically populate this Quick Access menu with the scripts we've written so far: ToggleShowAllFiles and BBEditMail.

To do this, we simply have to place the script files into a folder called Scripts in our home directory Library folder. We need to create it first – so using a quick keyboard combination we'll do a Shift+Command+G (for Go) in Finder and type in ~/Library. From there we'll do a Shift+Command+N (for New folder) and name it Scripts.

Now we'll copy the two script files from our Desktop to the scripts directory as thus:

Now with those files present, if we select the Script menu bar item we'll see them in the menu!

The beauty of this method is that if we select the script name, it is automatically parsed and executed. The editor isn't launched nor is the file loaded and displayed – it is simply the immediate execution of the script.

This is a very easy and powerful way for you to perform any number of script jobs directly from your menu bar and I highly recommend you dig into how much you can get done in this manner.

ENCRYPTED DISK IMAGES

Data security had been my primary career for over 25 years. It wasn't until recently that I gave up on the security field after watching it deteriorate from the true practice of IT security into what is now simply "compliance." In the few years I worked for Microsoft I directly experienced the purposeful abandonment of working towards actually *being* secure in favor of the much more simple practice of just *saying* you're secure whether you were or not.

I'll give you a quick analogy. Let's say you need to get homeowners' insurance, and one of the criteria to qualify is that you have to have locks on all your doors. The insurance company asks if you do, and you say "yes." So you get insurance.

But what you didn't tell the insurance company is that none of the windows even have glass in them, and they are just wide, gaping holes in the house than anyone can just climb into.

Is your home secure? Of course not, and you know it. But the insurance company didn't ask about the windows, and you chose not to tell them. All they required is that you had locks on your front doors, so that's all you did, and all you're going to do.

That's the difference between being secure and saying you're secure. And that's why I left Microsoft, which was the initial catalyst for me abandoning all Microsoft systems and software and switching to Apple. We were supposed to be on the Road to Damascus, but it turned out to be more like Dumbasskiss.

So where is this leading? I'm going to show you a very powerful yet easy way to protect your data but to have the option of full portability and backup.

This will be by way of creating an encrypted disk image with tools built directly into OS X.

If you are familiar with Windows, you may know of what is called EFS (encrypted file system) or BitLocker. EFS is a way of encrypting files in particular directories, but it is extremely unwieldy and difficult to use properly. You can also (easily) permanently lose access to your data by simply moving files around or changing users. I actually wrote an entire chapter in Thor's Microsoft Security Bible around EFS and WebDav to show administrators how to properly use EFS and how to ensure they didn't screw things up.

BitLocker is a utility that allows you to encrypt entire drives, but as Windows is really "cripple-ware," you have to purchase Enterprise or Ultimate versions to even have access to it. And even so, you can only encrypt entire drives and you can again do things that will forever scramble your data.

What we are going to cover here is a simple, powerful, and secure way of keeping particular data files safe, and we'll do so by introducing OS X's "Disk Utility" application.

But first I'll just explain the overall process.

While File Vault allows us to encrypt our entire drives (in a better and more usable way than BitLocker), what I think is of far more utility is to create a disk image which we will encrypt. This will basically be a single file of a given size which, when opened, will actually mount as a separate drive. When mounted, the image will present itself as would any other drive; we can then copy files to it, or edit files already on it.

Once we eject that drive image, it simply closes and once again resides as an encrypted file on your file system, which can be free copied around without the worry of its access being bound to a particular user account or dependencies upon other files or processes on your system. It will be a fully independent, secure file.

You can certainly use other utilities to do this, such as the free TruCrypt utility available for many operating systems, but that requires you to install that utility on all systems from which you want access to the data.

With an encrypted disk image, you can open the file securely from any Mac system you choose without installing anything. Cool beans.

This is an extremely easy process. First launch Disk Utility – you'll see the main Disk Utility window. Mine looks like this:

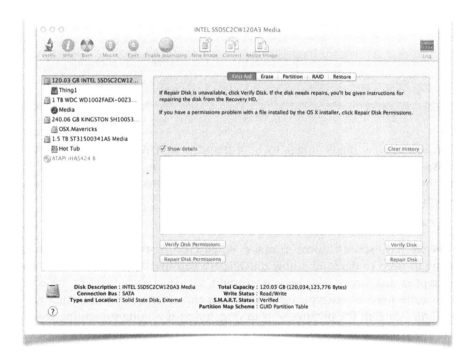

Using the top menu bar Disk Utility drop-down menu, we'll select File -> New -> Blank Disk Image.

This gives the following dialog box.

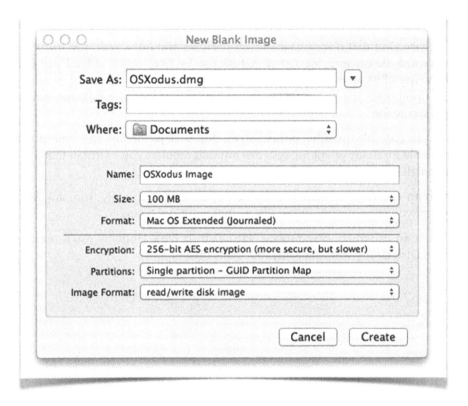

Consider a New Blank Image to be a brand new hard drive you just pur-chased. You're going to have to format it in a certain manner, and, depending on the OS, you will have options regarding partitions, their size, and even whether they are going to be encrypted or not.

OS X supports all of these options.

Now we have some choices to make. When creating the disk image, you're going to need to determine how much space you need. Since this will be an encrypted disk image, our use-case should take into account only the data you really need to encrypt. I don't recommend creating an image that will accommodate all the pictures of your dog, unless it's doing something really, really bad and you can't have anyone see it.

For me, once I thought about exactly what I wanted to accomplish, I was able to determine that the most important files – or rather, the most sensitive – could all be saved on a 200-meg disk image.

This of course is based on *my* needs – yours will be different. But I had a few other considerations I had to take into account.

For one, I store my encrypted disk images in the cloud. There's no way in hell that I would put sensitive files in any cloud service without them being encrypted.

While some services, such as AWS, allow you to store your files (e.g. a service called S3) and encrypt those files, the key to decrypt them is actually stored within the AWS infrastructure. I have to assume that if someone hacked the AWS services to the point they could get to my S3 file system that they could also get to the keys.

Storing keys where you store your data is, in my opinion, retarded. It's like locking your front door but leaving the key in the lock.

When storing files in the cloud, size is a consideration. The bigger the file, the higher the cost – both in storage fees and in time and bandwidth to access the data.

I get 20 gig "free" with my paid subscription to Adobe Creative Cloud, and that's a good amount of storage. As part of that service, Creative Cloud's file synchronization feature allows me to seamlessly and autonomously synchronize the files I have stored in the cloud with my laptop. When I work on files on my office rig, the moment I connect my laptop to the internet those files are synchronized down to my MacBook Pro.

Part of this file sync includes my encrypted disk images. Therefore, I've been very conscious of file size to ensure data transfer is quick and complete, even when at Starbucks or some other place where bandwidth is limited.

If you don't have these considerations, then there's no problem creating a multi-gig image. Sixteen-gig USB drives are a dime a dozen these days, and you can store a lot of data on them. To be clear, if I had a 16-gig memory stick I was going to put encrypted data on, I'd just encrypt the entire stick. But if you are going to be copying your disk image around, that's a bit of a different animal.

Regardless, in this example, I'm going to go ahead and leave the default Size of 100 MB. Make sure you change the actual "Name" field as well (not just the file name). This Name will be displayed later when you mount the image. The important part for us here is the "Encryption" option. We have two choices – AES128 and AES256. Both use the same encryption algorithm, but they use different key sizes. Let's go back to our lock analogy; in general locks work by having pin tumblers in the plug align with the upper pins along the shear line. The key cut is what makes these pins align.

As regards picking a lock, the more pins, the harder to pick. A three-pin lock is far easier to pick than a five-pin lock.

For purposes of this analogy, consider AES128 a lock with 128 pins and AES256 a lock with 256 pins. The lock itself is of the same construction, but the one with 256 pins is far harder to pick.

Going back to our disk image, AES128 is still an extremely secure algorithm. In fact, I'd wager that most of the SSL (HTTPS) sites you visit are still using AES128 to encrypt the data. This is because encrypting data with AES128 is faster and takes less CPU time than using AES256. With web sites and transferring data over the wires, speed and resource allocation is a huge consideration. As always, security gets trumped by business considerations.

Your only consideration here is that AES128 encryption is faster than AES256 encryption. As it relates to copying and editing your data files, I would venture to say that you'll never even perceive the difference on any modern computer. Therefore, I recommend using AES256 as I do to ensure that your data will, as far as we know, never be cracked in your lifetime. Or that of your great-great-great-great-great-grandchild. I actually could have put about a thousand "great's" but my editor would probably get irritated with me.

After naming your image and selecting AES256, you just click "Create" to begin the process. I've named mine OSXodus. OS now prompts us to enter a password to encrypt and decrypt the data. AES (Advanced Encryption Standard) is a "symmetric" encryption algorithm, which means the same password both encrypts and decrypts the data. PKI (public key infrastructure) (as explained in Chapter 5, OS X Server) initially uses the RSA (Rivest-Shamir-Adelman) algorithm to encrypt and decrypt data – however, RSA is asymmetric, which means a different key encrypts the data than the one that decrypts the data; this is the public key and private key, respectively.

The password you choose is important. Let's talk about that for a moment. Unfortunately, it seems the security world has fully embraced the concept that a "complex" password is a "strong" password. This is a myth. Particularly when it comes to symmetric encryption, *length* is the most important part of a password. Actually, we'll be using a *passphrase*.

Your bank makes you use a password with uppercase letters, lowercase letters, and numbers. They may even make you use a "special" character like a $ or & symbol. This is really, really silly as you only get a few chances to logon before your account is locked out. If my password to my bank was "garbage," the chances of someone actually guessing that in would be next to nil.

In contrast, using "garbage" as your AES password would be a really, really BAD idea. The difference is between *online* cracking and *offline* cracking. With online cracking, the entity you are trying to logon to owns the access controls. They can lock you out, they can get your IP, they can do whatever they want.

However, with offline cracking, as would be the case if I got hold of your encrypted disk image, you can't control what I do. I can put a brute force tool against your file and try password after password from a "dictionary" and if that didn't work I'd just brute force it starting with "a" and going through the entire keyspace. If you are interested in this type of thing, I suggest you visit my Password Machine at http://www.hammerofgod.com/passwordmachine.php.

Looking at the password "garbage," a seven character lower-case password, it would take an attacker 2.18 seconds to break your encryption if they were using what's called "Class F" brute force speeds. That's at a billion attempts per second. Yes, that's crazy fast and only a handful of folks would have access to that manner of brute forcing, but it's out there so we have to plan for worst case, because the iterations required to get to "garbage" is only two billion, one hundred and eighty-two million, five hundred and fifty-three thousand, three hundred and ninety-one. Here's more info:

Primary Stats	Additional Stats	
Your Pwd	garbage	
Pwd Length	7 (seven)	
MD5	c8e8df895c2cae166bad027fdf15335b	Google Lookup
SHA1	78c67c126575c20c6b468447355e9bd20d221202	Google Lookup
BF-Class	1,000,000,000 (one billion) per-second.	
BF-Base	26 (twenty-six): abcdefghijklmnopqrstuvwxyz	
Pwd Iterations	2,182,553,391 (Scientific notation of: 2.182553e+9)	
	two billion, one hundred and eighty-two million, five hundred and fifty-three thousand, three hundred and ninety-one.	
Time-to-Crack	Seconds: 2.18	

Most security folks would have you enter a passphrase with all manner of complex upper case, lowercase, special characters and randomized numbers. While this level of "keyspace" does indeed make the passphrase harder to brute force, it makes it harder for you to remember. When you can't remember something, you write it down.

At Microsoft, I was having this exact conversation with someone in compliance in a different group. This is a true story. He said there's no way I could ever get his Bitlocker password because it was "complex." I reached over and lifted up his keyboard, and there, on a piece of paper, was his freaking password. I swear.

So let's consider a passphrase that is easy to remember but "impossible" to crack: "my dog ate a clown." You can remember that for the rest of your life, but it would never be cracked by a dictionary attack because those attacks don't (and effectively can't) concatenate words into random phrases.

If you were going to try to brute force this passphrase, even though it is all lowercase, it would take 1,469,296,259,960,773,632 YEARS to crack the password at Class F speeds. That's one quintillion, four hundred sixty-nine quadrillion, two hundred ninety-six trillion, two hundred fifty-nine billion, nine hundred sixty million, seven hundred seventy-three thousand, six hundred thirty-two years, if you didn't feel like figuring it out.

To put it in perspective, that is 106,470,743,475 (106 trillion) times the age of the universe.

The reason is because, with that length of password, again even if you only use the 26 lowercase letters of the alphabet, the number of iterations required to arrive at that combination of letters (with the spaces, of course) would be one hundred and thirty-seven decillion, one hundred and forty-eight nonillion, four hundred and eighty-three octillion, five hundred and thirty-three septillion, nine hundred and seventy-seven sextillion, two hundred and sixty-one quintillion, eight hundred and seventy-eight quadrillion, one hundred and six trillion, five hundred and thirty-nine billion, four hundred and ninety-two million, nine hundred thousand, eight hundred and sixty-four.

That's a bunch. I don't know about you, but given this, I'm fine with "my dog ate a clown" as my passphrase. Besides, clowns should in fact be eaten by dogs because they're creepy.

Using that passphrase we see this:

We see that our passphrase is "Excellent." That's good. However, what I don't think is good is the fact that Disk Utility has "Remember password in my key-chain" enabled by default.

Uncheck this. Well, do what you want, but 'twer I you, I would uncheck it. If you ask Disk Utility to store the passphrase in your keychain, when you go to mount the image, KeyChain Access will automatically provide it to the DiskImage Mounter without prompting you. This means that if anyone got into your machine logged on as you, they could mount your encrypted drive without knowing the password.

Unchecking this option ensures that, no matter where you are or who you are logged in as, the DiskImage Mounter will ask for your password to mount the image.

Now, no matter what machine we are on, even if on a Mac in an internet cafe somewhere (assuming you have your image on a stick or equivalent) you will always be prompted for your passphrase when you attempt to mount the .dmg file.

When we successfully enter our decryption passphrase, OS X will mount the image as a drive, where we can put whatever files we want (limited by disk space, of course).

You can edit directly from this mounted image just as you do from your hard drives or USB sticks. The difference is that as you write data, the underlying image file data is encrypted with AES256. When you eject this image and it closes, your file data will be secure and can only be mounted with your passphrase. This is why it's important to understand how password "strength" manifests itself and why you should make sure you can remember your passphrase without writing it down. If you forget it, there's no way you can ever recover your data.

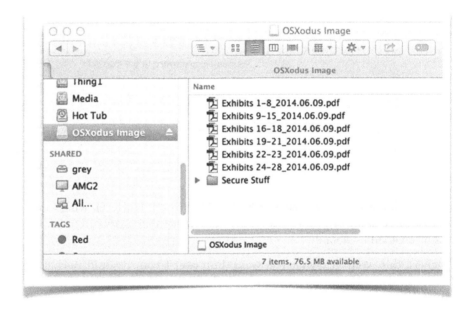

INTELLIGENT, MULTI-CHOICE DIALOG BOXES

This will only take a moment to explain, but I find it a very valuable feature. In Windows, when presented with a dialog box, you'll always have a single, default option. For instance, when you get a confirmation box to do something, you may get "Yes, No, Cancel" options with "Yes" as the default. You can either click it or hit the Enter key to accept the default. Of course, if you don't want "Yes" you have to tab through or click the item you want.

OS X dialog boxes are a bit more intelligent: they give you a "default" option but also give you a "secondary default" option. Meaning, if one hits Enter, the default option is selected; however, if you hit the space bar, the secondary option is selected.

Take a new Apple Mail message as an example. If I'm editing a new message but decide to close it, Mail will present me with the following dialog box:

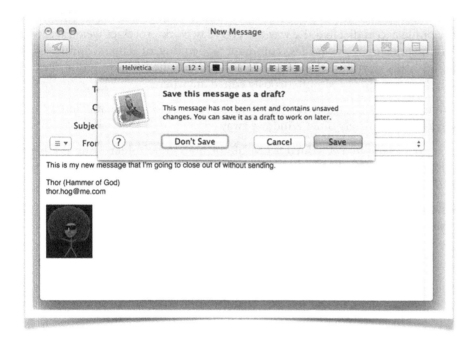

Examine the options. The "Save" button is fully shaded in blue. Those reading the printed copy will just see grey, of course, but it's blue. Hitting the Enter key on your keyboard will save the mail item as a Draft.

But look at the "Don't Save" button. You'll see it outlined in blue. This means that if you hit your Space bar on the keyboard, that mail will close the item without saving it as a draft. It may sound like a trivial feature, but I use this a hundred times a day, easily. Not with just mail, of course, but throughout my daily OS X experience.

Learning various keyboard combinations to perform operations you would normally use your mouse for will greatly enhance your experience and speed up execution of typical functions.

INTELLIGENT SHARED FILE SYSTEM UPDATES

When I first discovered this feature in OS X, I was amazed. I have gotten so used to the file system behavior in Windows that this really blew my mind.

Let's say I open a text file in Windows Notepad and begin editing it. If I try to edit that file in any other program I'll get an "access denied" because the file is in use. There's nothing I can do with that file (other than maybe use the "type" command in a DOS window) because Notepad is using it. This manner of file access dictated the way my everyday work processes were executed. Any manner of copying files, automatic appending of data, scripting, editing or really anything else was designed and executed knowing that files in Windows couldn't be simultaneously edited anywhere.

Not only is this not true with OS X, but OS X provided automatic update features that completely blow Windows away.

Take this example. I've edited a text file in my Home folder using the bash utility "nano." We discuss nano in Chapter 4, OS Xodus: Remote Access – SSH Supplement.

I created a text file named "thor.txt" and saved it. It contains the following text:

```
This is my text file originally created using Nano.
I've saved it as thor.txt
```

I then exited out of nano and my bash prompt and loaded up a wonderful application called BBEdit and opened up the thor.txt file.

I added some dashes to the file along with some text and saved the file in BBEdit. It now looks like this:

```
This is my text file originally created using Nano.
I've saved it as thor.txt
---------
I'm now editing in BBEdit. I'm going to save and go
back into Nano and add something.
---------
```

Here's where the magic comes in. While the file was still open in BBEdit, I went back to my bash prompt and executed a "nano thor.txt" file to bring it up in edit mode. I then added a line of text and saved the file, which resulted in the file now containing:

```
This is my text file originally created using Nano.
I've saved it as thor.txt
---------
```

```
I'm now editing in BBEdit. I'm going to save and go
back into Nano and add something.
---------
This was added back in Nano and saved.
```

Not only was I able to save the file in nano, but without touching anything, the last bit of text I added in nano **automatically** updated in my BBEdit window.

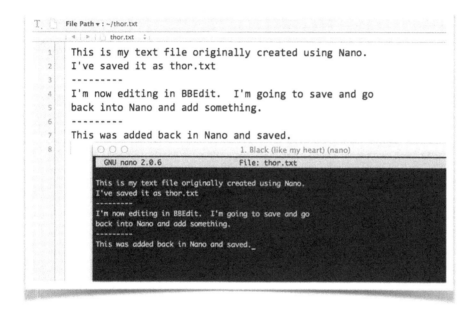

The file-update operating system event was fired and BBEdit's contents automatically displayed the results. This provides some really amazing functionality and is something Windows couldn't even dream of doing.

So let's explore some actual, practical applications of this functionality.

With multiple systems, there are times that I want to view what's going on on another box. For instance, my system Grey is a server, and I very well may want to see the log activity of that system. In Windows I'd have to go into Event View and connect up to another system which would have to be on the same LAN or accessible via VPN or some such nonsense. Of course remote management features would have to be turned on to do this, and accessing a remote box directly over the internet was nigh impossible unless you completely opened up all manner of ports and forwarded them to some box.

In OS X we can do this in a completely secure manner via SSH while taking full advantage of the operating system's automatic file-change update features. So let's do that using a combination of SSH, a command called "tail," and the Console application on our local machine.

"Tail" has been used in Unix and Linux boxes for many decades. It's a tried and true utility that grabs the last few lines (configurable in command-line switches) of a file and outputs that data to the standard output.

If I executed "tail" against the thor.txt file, since tail by default returns the last 10 lines of a file, we'll see the full file contents displayed in our bash session:

But tail also has the capability of continuously monitoring a file knowing that the *nix-based operating systems provide this type of function by default.

With this in mind, what we're going to do is establish a SSH session with our Grey server and execute a tail command to monitor Grey's http server log. However, what we're going to do is redirect the output of the tail through the SSH channel back to my own machine and stream it into a local file called "remote-httpd.log."

I'll then open up Console app, which is what we use to monitor our own local log files. Since our "remote-httpd.log" will already be in a Console log format, we will be able to monitor our remote Grey httpd log in real time. Even though the remote-httpd.log file will be open by the terminal prompt, being constantly updated by the tail command on the remote server via our

SSH channel, Console will be able to immediately update itself with the data being streamed down. Super cool.

This is a lot easier than it sounds and the entire process of piping back the log results can be done in a single bash command. The overall SSH process is covered in the Advanced section of the Remote Access chapter (Chapter 4) if you would like to review it. Here's the bash command:

```
ssh thor@grey.local "tail -f /var/log/apache2/access_log" >> ~/
remote-httpd.log
```

Again, this establishes the shell, executes a tail command against Apache's access log file, and pipes the results back through the SSH channel and into a file in my home directory called "remote-httpd.log."

One thing to remember is that you need to keep your bash shell open. Once you close it, the connection will terminate and the log file will no longer be updated.

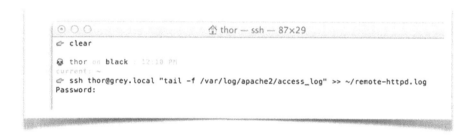

This will now create the log file in my home directory:

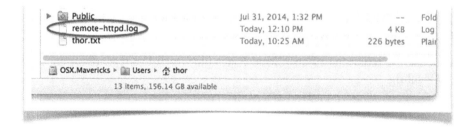

As long as the shell is open, remote-httpd.log will constantly update. If I double-click on the file, since I've used the .log extension, Console App will launch, open the log file, and begin displaying access log entries and will update in real time as new entries are created as the web service on Grey is accessed.

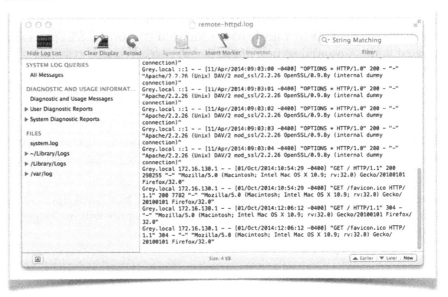

As you can see, though we're accessing our local remote-httpd.log file, the entries being updated are from "Grey.local."

Now I can just watch as folks access my web server. No special ports had to be opened on the server as only the SSH server (via the "Remote Logon" Sharing option as discussed in Remote Access) is being used. The transfer of log data is completely secure as it is all piped through the encrypted SSH channel. And the data is live.

Try that with Windows!!!

This live-update feature also works when you rename files – which is another feature Windows can't handle.

Let's use the renaming of an iCloud Pages file which I've recently opened on my local rig.

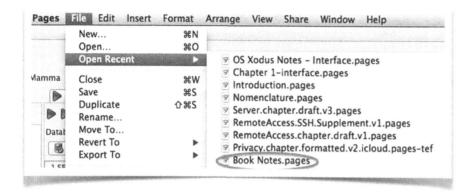

You'll note I've opened "Book Notes" recently in Pages. This document is actually stored in iCloud so that I have direct access to it from anywhere. I could have used the aforementioned Creative Cloud File Sync feature to do this, but that only works on two computers. iCloud storage also allows me to access that file on my iPhone and iPad since I have Pages loaded on those as well.

Now check THIS out. On my *laptop*, named BloodRed, and not my main rig where the preceding screenshot was taken, I'm going to go to All My Files and find the "Book Notes" file – my laptop has iCloud enabled so I can see the same file.

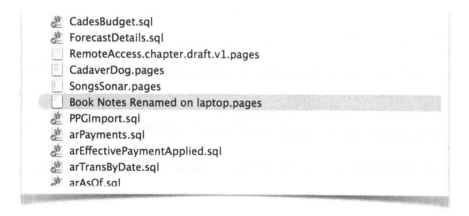

I do a lot of business work on my laptop, and you can see my documents folder has a lot of different documents – but you see I've renamed "Book Notes" to "Book Notes Renamed on laptop.pages."

If I now go back to my main rig (Black, Like My Heart) and simply pull up my Recents menu item in Pages again, this is what I see:

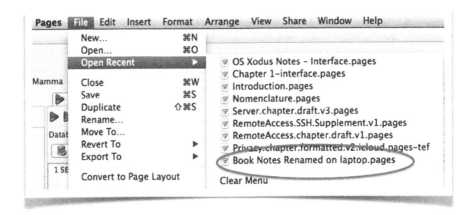

Even if I rename a file stored in the cloud from a different computer, OS X is smart enough to know this and it automatically changed the name for me, amazingly enough, in something so far removed as my Recent documents.

I can change the name of an Excel spreadsheet in my own Documents folder in Windows and will receive an error when I go to pull it up from Recents.

INTELLIGENT FILE COPY

Again, this is one of those quickies, but it is something that I find to be a huge benefit, and something that has bothered me in Windows for decades.

And that's the way the operating systems go about copying files.

I'm a big music buff, and have over 45,000 songs in my local library. It's enough music for me to listen to at work 8 hours a day, 5 days a week straight for almost 2 years without listening to the same song twice. And it's not just represented by 45k files, as I've got album art and other files that go along with the music.

When I'm updating a backup, trying to merge backups, or copy selected music to a USB drive or something, with this many files I'm bound to have a duplicate somewhere. And as you can imagine, the time it takes to complete these backups can be significant.

Here's the problem with Windows: When Windows performs a copy operation, it starts from the source file selection and begins copying the files to the destination. No matter how many files you select or where you copy them to, this is how it goes about it.

The problem is that Windows doesn't (and can't) determine if there is a file with the same name on the target *until it gets to it in the list of files as it copies them*. This results in you starting a copy operation, and at some point during the copy, the copy is interrupted and Windows just sits there waiting on you to confirm an overwrite or merge transaction.

I can't tell you the number of times I've started a large copy and gone off to do something else only to return to find Windows stopped at the point a file already exists, waiting for me to click "Yes" or "Skip." There are times when I've figured it got about 10 minutes into a 3-hour copy and screwed up my schedule.

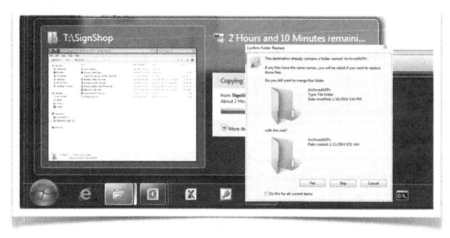

This is a shot of me in a substantial copy at work to a backup share. It may be hard to read, but there are 2 hours left after a substantial amount of time already passed where it stopped to ask me to confirm. It's a complete pain in the ass and a waste of my time.

OS X, on the other hand, is smart enough to check to see if there are any existing filename conflicts on the target *before* it starts actually copying the data. What a concept, huh?

As a test, I've selected almost 80 gig worth of music I've copied into one folder and am going to copy it all into another folder where the only common music folder is Oingo Boingo. I've got A-H and then T-W in the destination (along with Oingo Boingo) and am copying in J-S. That way I know I'll only have the "O" conflict.

While Windows would copy A-H and then error at O, here's what I immediately (and I mean *immediately*) get from OS X:

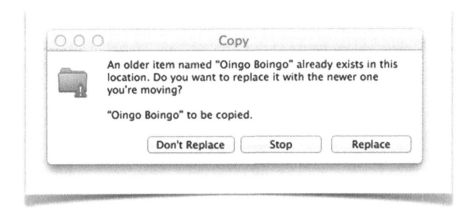

Since the test directory was created after the original, it not only warns me it exists, but tells me the source is newer than the destination.

Any other conflicts which may exist will also be handled up-front before the copy operation takes place, so you can leave with confidence that when you return, your job will have completed without interruption.

Another superior feature of OS X file copy operations is the "up-front" creation of directories and folder-based progress reporting.

In Windows, if you are sitting by the target directory during a copy operation, you only see folders as they are actually created by the copy process. And the overall copy progress is a single, overall progression bar.

When copying files in OS X, you are immediately presented with what folders will be created in the target directory, and are given progress bars on a *folder-by-folder* basis!

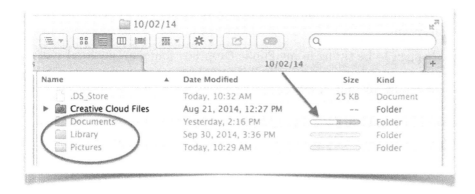

As you sit in the target folder, you'll see folders to be created greyed out, and each with their own progress bar. As the folders (and their contents) are copied over, they change to the standard 100% opacity list views.

You can see that, as I make my backup copy of data to my USB drive, the Documents, Library, and Pictures folders have yet to have all files copied over to them and are greyed out. But you can also see that my Documents copy is about half done and that the other folders have not yet begun to copy. This is great information to have.

In fact, this functionality isn't limited to folders. If I am looking at a file-by-file list, it too provides me with progress on each file. In this example, I'm copying a bunch of SQL Server database backup files which are nontrivial in size. OS X shows me the progress on each:

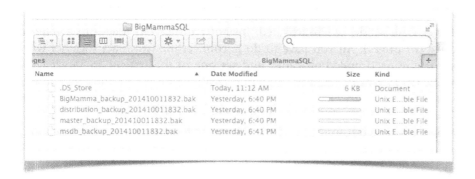

This provides me with all the information I could want for the progress of my copy operations.

But note that this behavior doesn't only exist during copy operations on my local system.

If I happen to be sitting in my Public Drop Box folder on my local system, and a remote system (my laptop in this case) begins a copy operation, OS X is smart enough to know it should update my local Finder view of the Drop Box to represent that a folder has been created and that data is currently being copied into it. Here I'm copying data from the Photoshop folder on my laptop to Thor's Public Drop Box on the host Black (Like My Heart):

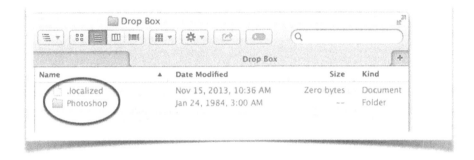

You'll note that during this process the Photoshop directory is greyed out even though the copy operation was initiated from a different, remote system connected over the network. As a side note, the ".localized" file is only visible because I'm showing hidden files as previously discussed.

While we're on the subject of copying files, I want to talk about a really cool way OS X allows you to very easily copy files directly between two Macs without having to set up networking, sharing or muck about with USB sticks or drives. It's called "Target Disk Mode" and it is a very cool feature.

Target Disk Mode, when activated, instantly turns your Mac into a remote drive (or drives). All you have to do is connect the two Macs together with a Firewire or Thunderbolt cable, and set one of the systems to Target Disk Mode (in System Preferences -> Startup Disk). Upon restart, the drives in the system set in Target Disk Mode will automatically appear in the other Mac's "Devices" in Finder. In this example, I put my MacBook Pro in Target Disk Mode, connected it to my iMac via Thunderbolt, and restarted the MacBook.

Upon restart, the drive on my laptop (named OS X) immediately showed up in my Finder window:

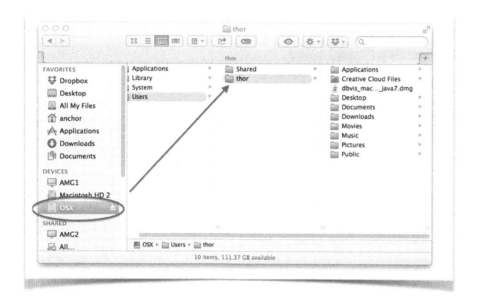

I can now copy files between the two systems as if I were copying data from one drive to another. In fact, when I took the preceding screenshot on the iMac, I simply copied it over to my OS X "drive" so I would have it paste it here. And with Thunderbolt I can do it at 10 gigabits per second!

When you're done copying files, simply restart the Target system and it boots right back up into OS X. Awesome.

Yet again it's the obvious and simple functionality that OS X provides that makes it so much better. The main takeaway here isn't just the fact these cool features are in place in singularity – these features represent a presence of mind and attention to detail that simply don't exist anywhere in the Windows development process. I know. I've been there.

By the way, that isn't a knock against the Windows developers themselves – there are some very, very bright and talented people who work at Microsoft. It's the overall management and development process which renders them impotent that is the real problem.

CHAPTER 4

OS Xodus: Remote Access

With everyone moving to "The Cloud," having remote access to your data may not seem like a big deal. However, I think it's important to understand the difference between what I'm defining as "Remote Access" to your data and simply "Shared" or "Centralized Access" to data stored in cloud services.

For the purposes of this chapter, when I discuss Remote Access, it means you gaining access to systems, services, and data on resources which *you* own and control, from a remote location. The distinction, of course, is that once you store data in the cloud, you no longer have control over the data. You might be able to tell the cloud services with whom to share your data, and where, within some manner of directory structure, to put the data; but you don't really *control* the data. The cloud provider does. Your only "control" of the data is via what interface and access controls the provider decides to give you.

But they own control of the actual data. They control the servers. They control the connection they provide to you. And they own the "security" of the data insofar as the overall cloud service is concerned.

By way of example, let's take Microsoft Azure Cloud Services. Even though the word "azure" is defined as the color of a sky with no clouds, we'll dance over the ramifications of such a moniker and move on. Many (not all) of the Azure services are provided by way of Hyper-V virtualization servers. These servers are, in turn, running Microsoft Server operating systems. This means your data is being stored on servers, via services, that you have no control over. You don't know how many administrators have full access to your data. In fact (and I know this directly, first hand), Microsoft doesn't even know how many administrators have access to your data. In general, Microsoft internally has an incredibly difficult time making sure systems get patched and updated. Publicly available servers can sometimes go months without being patched.

What this means for you is that, without knowing it, your data could be exposed to any number of people at any time.

CONTENTS

VNC 124

Apple Remote Desktop 127

iCloud's Back to My Mac 137

SSH Supplement – Advanced Section 148

To be fair, this overall paradigm is an issue for all cloud services. But in the case of Microsoft, you've got a far higher rate of vulnerability exposure. And exploitation of these vulnerabilities. You've also got availability and performance issues that you wouldn't have if the cloud provider were using more secure and stable operating systems.

An example of this would be Hyper-V virtualization, versus VMWare virtualization services. To run Hyper-V, you first have to perform an installation of Windows Server. Then you enable Hyper-V, and then you configure your virtual machines. VMWare's ESX product boots directly into its own operating system, where you can begin your configurations. This means that the ESX model is immediately more secure, as there is no concern for the massive number of people out in the world attacking the lower hanging fruit of Microsoft services.

The same goes for Azure versus Amazon Web Services. Amazon uses the Linux Xen platform for virtualization. The functionality and security of the Xen Project is contributed to not only by Amazon, but by Cisco, Google, Intel, Oracle, and even Samsung.

While there was a time that iCloud used Azure for storing certain data encrypted by iCloud services, Apple, too, has embraced the power, availability, and security of Amazon Web Services.

Now that I've appropriately chastised Microsoft as a converted One Who Has Seen The Light, to move on, remember that, when it comes to the data you and I store in the cloud, we are still at the mercy of how the provider chooses to store and secure that data.

In this chapter we will be discussing how you will gain access to YOUR data stored on YOUR systems.

I'll basically be discussing two different remote access models. The first will be in regard to services such as Virtual Network Computing (VNC) and Apple Remote Desktop (ARD), which allow you to have a full graphic interface where you control the remote computer as if you were sitting at its desktop.

Secondly, we'll discuss access to your data as if it were just another data source in your Finder window. Included will be access to files from your iPad or iPhone via Virtual Private Network (VPN) services.

VNC

Virtual Network Computing, or VNC, is an open source application that provides screen sharing services and is available for virtually all operating systems such as Windows, Linux, and of course OS X.

VNC is the core application at the heart of OS X screen sharing and Apple Remote Desktop, herein referred to as ARD. While the ARD client provides a far greater range of functionality, I am specifically carving out the VNC server functions in this section, so you know that you can use any of the many VNC clients to connect to your Mac. The ARD client is a for-purchase application from the App Store.

The main reason I'm covering VNC here is that we all must accept the fact that business requirements will mostly likely force you to use a Windows system at some point, if not constantly. And, of course, you very well may have a mixture of Windows and OS X simply because you choose to, which is great.

If you need to connect to your OS X screen via a Windows computer, this functionality is provided right out of the box in OS X via the VNC server service.

I'm going to assume that you've already got some manner of VNC client on your Windows machine such as TightVNC or UltraVNC. Some are free and some are for-pay, but I'm going to leave it up to you to install and configure those clients.

Configuring VNC server services in OS X is extremely easy. In your System Preferences app, you'll go to the Sharing option and turn on Remote Management, as shown here.

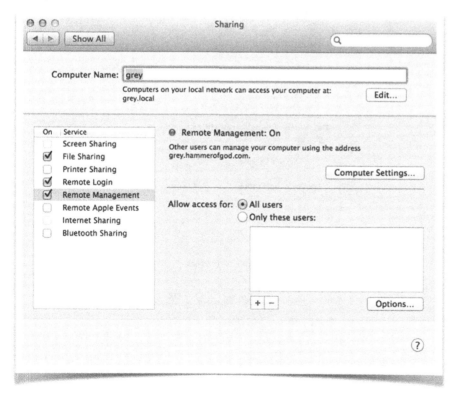

You'll see in my configuration I've got three server services configured: File Sharing (which enables me to share my directories on the local network), Remote Login, and Remote Management. Remote Login enables an SSH server, allowing one to directly connect to a shell, via an SSH or SFTP client. We'll discuss those in a bit, but it is the Remote Management service we need to enable the VNC service.

And guess what? We're done. You can now connect to your OS X system securely with your Windows VNC client.

On a quick note, if you want to set up a VNC server on your Windows side and connect to the remote desktop from OS X, there's no need for any extra software. The "Screen Sharing" application acts as a VNC client for any VNC server.

You can't directly execute the Screen Sharing app from Finder, but you can easily invoke it by opening up a browser and specifying the VNC protocol by typing **vnc://** in the URL. This will open the "Launch Application" applet and allow you to specify Screen Sharing. From there you can connect to whatever you want.

It should also be noted that if you wish to connect to your OS X box via a VNC client or Screen Sharing client from outside your network, you'll need to forward TCP port 5900 to your internal OS X box. That may be an obvious point, but I wanted to make sure it was stated.

APPLE REMOTE DESKTOP

When I first got started with OS X, I was a bit confused about how ARD worked. Coming from a Microsoft background, I thought I would have to install some manner of "ARD Server" in order to connect up to OS X via ARD.

The problem was that I was making things too hard, as I often did (and still do sometimes), because I was so used to configuring services in Windows. I've done substantial work with Remote Desktop Protocol, and was used to substantial configuration requirements to implement a secure RDP environment.

I finally figured out that the Remote Management service was all that was needed for one to use the ARD client. Meaning, I originally thought I had to install the ARD client on all the computers I wished to control. I was wrong – enabling Remote Management on the host is all that is necessary. I just needed the ARD client application installed that I wanted to control other hosts from.

As previously stated, remote management via screen sharing is included in the OS X installation, but if you want to take advantage of the power afforded by ARD you have to purchase the application from the App Store. To be fair, both the RDP server and client components are included in Windows installations. The RDP functionality from a Windows client has many more features than OS X's standard screen sharing, but the ARD client dwarfs the RDP client insofar as remote capabilities are concerned. ARD allows you to do things like instant remote Spotlight Searches, perform robust file transfers, execute remote commands, and even install software on your OS X installations remotely.

You can consider ARD to be a full remote management tool for all your systems and a client appropriate even for larger business installations, and it only costs $79 USD. This is better illustrated by the following screenshot showing the ARD client main menu:

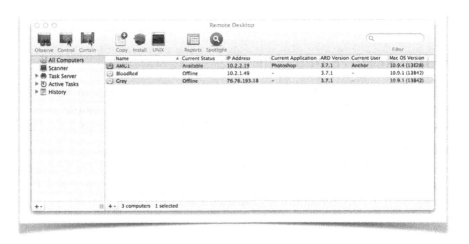

The ARD interface allows you to scan your entire network for computers to automatically populate a list of the computers on your network. You can, of course, manually enter other hosts; this would be required to connect to systems outside of your network, as you can see in the case of my "Grey" host. Part of the interface tells you the current user logged on, IP address, the system status, and even what application that box is currently running.

Let's explore a few of the functions ARD performs. The most obvious and popular is the actual remote control of the host I choose. I've set my preferences to double-click on the hostname to remotely control it. Doing so gives me full control of the remote box and I get a full screen view.

In this case, I've taken over the OS X box I use for Photoshop work and video productions. The performance and graphic support is impressive. I can even watch video remotely, with no apparent degradation in video quality. This will, of course, depend upon what your available bandwidth is. There will be more information regarding screen sharing in the "Back-to-my-Mac" section of this chapter.

But let's say I wanted to just get information on a remote host, without having to open a screen sharing session on the remote host. In fact, let's further say I want to perform several functions on the remote host without having to interrupt the current user at all.

The first thing I want to see is some general information about that host. Selecting the "Reports" menu item gives us the following reporting options:

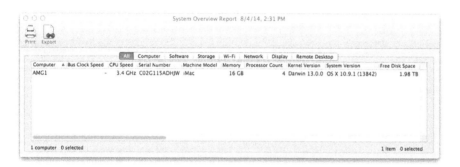

There is a wealth of data I can request, such as information on storage, sharing, host hardware configuration, and even what software is installed on that box. One should note that multiple computers can be selected all at once and ARD will go out and collect that data. In the screenshot, I've only the one host available on this network.

I now get detailed results, host-by-host, broken down and separated by tabs for Computer, Software, Storage, Wi-fi, Network, Display, and Remote Desktop. That's a bunch of information, and that was just the default information category selections. You can drill down into any of the categories to get even more information:

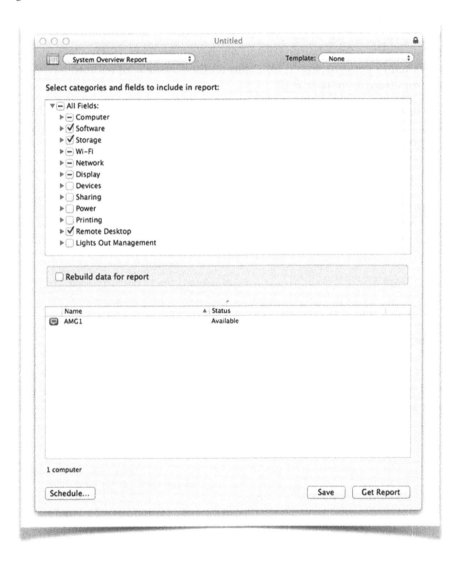

You can see how Remote Desktop can be used in large OS X environments to allow administrators to easily manage their resources.

Now, let's say we wanted to actively execute some UNIX commands on the remote host to get a directory listing of the home directory for the remote computer's currently logged on user. We could certainly connect via remote control of the screen, and go into Finder, but let's say we didn't want to interrupt the remote user; in fact, we don't want to use screen sharing at all.

This is where the power of ARD comes in. We'll simply click on the "UNIX" icon (or select "Send Unix Command" from the "Manage" command toolbar).

The "UNIX" command to get a directory listing is "ls". This would be a command you would enter in the Terminal app, or in my case the iTerm app. When a UNIX command is executed remotely via the Remote Desktop client, it invokes the command via /bin/bash on the remote system. As we can see, I've selected "ls ~/" which makes /bin/bash perform a "ls" command. The "~/" parameter indicates that I was asking for a directory listing of the current user's home directory.

Upon execution, I get the directory contents listed in a results window:

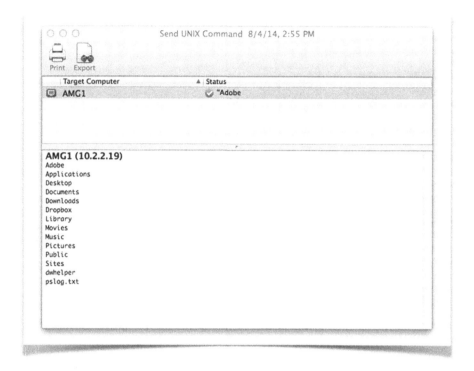

The contents of that user's home directory are now displayed. In this case, using "ls" as an example shows me that my graphic artist has installed "Dropbox" on that system, which I'm not actually happy about. But that's another story.

We can also move files around via Remote Desktop if we want. In this example, I'm an administrator who needs to be certain each of my hosts has a set of files on their local computer. Easy-peasy. The "Copy" command allows me to do this.

But before I do, I should search the remote systems to see if the files are already there, right? This is where remote Spotlight searching comes in. Selecting "Spotlight" gives me the following options:

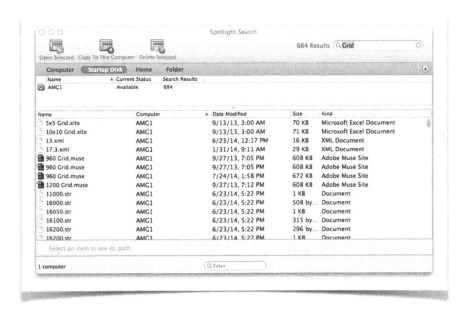

I've got several Grid files I want to search for, so I just ask ARD to perform a search for "Grid." It's important to note that my client is not reaching out and searching the storage of the remote host to perform this search – ARD is telling the remote host to execute its own spotlight search for Grid, and to return the results to me. This is super-cool as it ensures top performance with a minimal bandwidth cost.

Now I can get down to business and go to my "Copy" options to send whatever files I need to whichever hosts I want. Since I found the Grid files, all I need to do is send over an installation package.

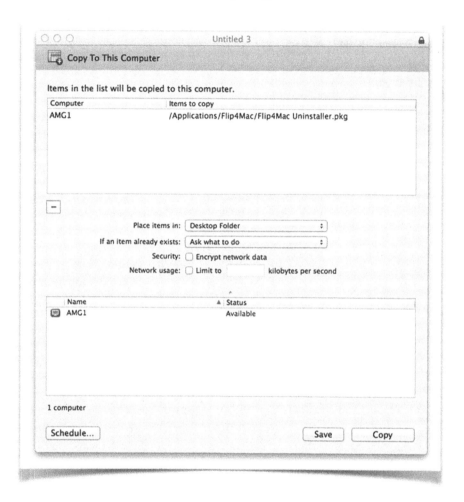

I've got many options available, such as where to put the files, whether or not to encrypt the files as they are being transferred, and even how much bandwidth to limit the transfer to. Very cool stuff.

Finally, let's say I want to use ARD to go out and install software on a bunch of servers. I simply select "Install" and choose my options.

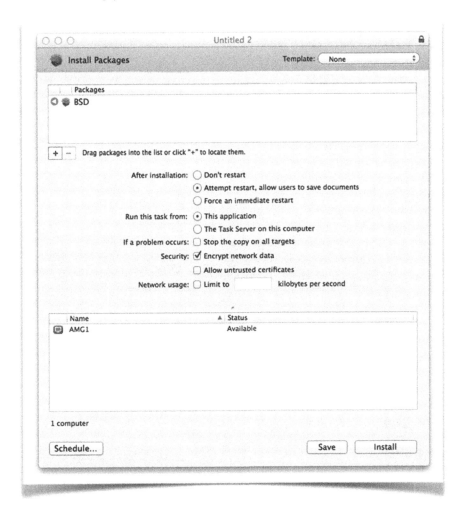

Again, I'm prompted with many options regarding the remote software installation. What's important to realize is the difference between what we're about to do with remote Install Package vs. the previous "Copy" command. When I copied the "Flip4Mac Uninstaller" package, it was my intent to have the user run the installation package from their desktop on their own. I simply copied the file there, and they can run it when they want to, directly from their desktop.

With the ARD "Install" option, the remote installation is performed *from my client*. It will basically stream the installation bits from the single "BSD" package on my system and install it on the remote hosts I specify. In this way, I don't have to copy any packages on the remote hosts. Everything is streamed down from my client to the remote host. This is why the "Network Usage" function (in the image above) is so cool – I can limit how much bandwidth is taken up by the installation stream so that other network functions don't suffer.

When you consider that the Microsoft solution (SMS) costs $799 just for a 25-client license, that should put the power of ARD into perspective. And that's the 2003 version! On that note, that solution requires a completely separate server solution with proprietary client software installation requirements. And that pricing doesn't include the server OS you have to purchase. Its stuff like this that makes me wish I switched to Apple, and open source products, years ago.

This pretty much wraps up the ARD section. Again, it is important to note that if you are going to enable ARD access to your resources from external connections that you will not only have to port forward TCP 5900 for the Screen Sharing functions, but you'll also need to forward TCP and UDP 3283, and TCP 5988 in order to use the enhanced features offered by Apple Remote Desktop.

iCLOUD'S BACK TO MY MAC

In my opinion, Back to My Mac offers the greatest level of functionality with the least exposure to security issues.

When enabled via your iCloud configuration, Back to My Mac allows you not only to remotely control your Mac via Screen Sharing, but it also allows you direct access to your shared files via Finder, as if they were another shared resource on your network. The best thing about these features is that they do not require you to explicitly open ports, as Back to My Mac uses special NAT features in combination with system connections to iCloud in order to automatically configure connections on demand when the service is being utilized. This is a major win for security as there are no static ports remaining open all the time.

For instance, there are tools available for an attacker to point to a host and perform a "brute force" attack against your VNC service, where it will repeatedly try to login as a particular user using passwords from a "dictionary list" over and over. If one was to have the password "duck" for the administrator account, such a tool would very quickly gain admin access to that account. This is because any client (unless you limit inbound connections by IP address) can connect to port 5900 from anywhere if your router is configured with a static port-forwarding rule as described in the VNC section of this chapter.

Back to My Mac handles this by routing connection requests through their Back to My Mac Servers which "broker" the connection request between the Macs you've enabled the services on. Not only is the connection between the Macs (and servers) encrypted with IPSec and SSL, but the authentication between iCloud accounts is secured with certificate-based Kerberos identity management. The client side certificates Back to My Mac uses to secure the authentication process are specific to your iCloud account, and are created when you enable iCloud. These certificates are part of your "System" certificates which you can view with the Keychain Access app as you can see under the "Kind" column.

Name	Kind
/Active Directory/	application password
134040459.members.btmm.icloud.com.	Back to My Mac key
134040459@p08–btmm.icloud.com:443	Back to My Mac key
134040459@p08–btmmdns.icloud.com:443	Back to My Mac key
134040459@p08–hello.connectivity.icloud.com:443	Back to My Mac key
Apple Worldwide Developer Relations Certification Authority	certificate
com.apple.kerberos.kdc	certificate
com.apple.kerberos.kdc	public key
com.apple.kerberos.kdc	private key
com.apple.systemdefault	certificate
com.apple.systemdefault	public key
com.apple.systemdefault	private key

As a long-time security professional, it is very satisfying to me to see a company implement such a strong encryption and authentication scheme into such an easy user interface. It would be really nice to see such features implemented by other operating systems.

To get started, all you have to do is to go into your iCloud configuration in System Preferences and turn on "Back to My Mac."

That's it! I know, it's amazing. Nothing this simple (or this functional) exists for Windows. The one thing you need to make sure of is that your router supports the required NAT functionality as per this message:

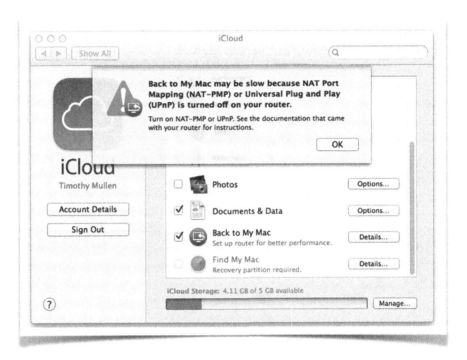

Most current routers support this functionality out of the box, but you might run into problems if trying to use Back to My Mac to connect to a Mac you've got in a corporate environment. There are a number of reasons for this, most of which revolve around corporate IT folks who don't understand NAT-PMP. That may sound a bit crass, but I've seen it many, many times. I've also seen where certain PNP features were disabled due to a massive vulnerability in Microsoft implementation of Plug and Play. Though not necessary, admins would disable PnP on everything, and not just the vulnerable Windows systems. Oh, well. For most of you using this, it won't be a problem at all.

Since both my systems at work and at home are configured to use Back to My Mac, my home system "Grey" shows up directly in my Finder "Shared" systems list even though it's not on my local network.

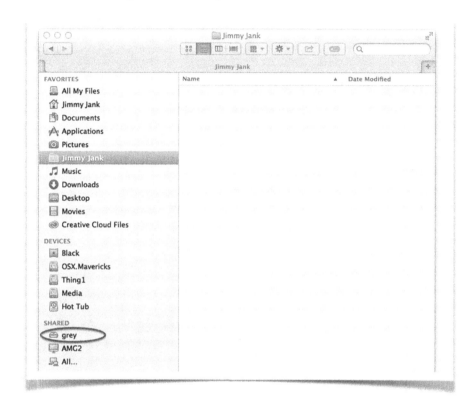

If I click on "grey" in my list (from my system Black at my office), the system will automatically try to connect using the current user context from your remote system. If you have configured "Automatic Logon" on your remote host, Back to My Mac will automatically logon and present you with a list of the shared resources on the host you've connected to. Automatic Logon is configured via "Users and Groups" in System Preferences:

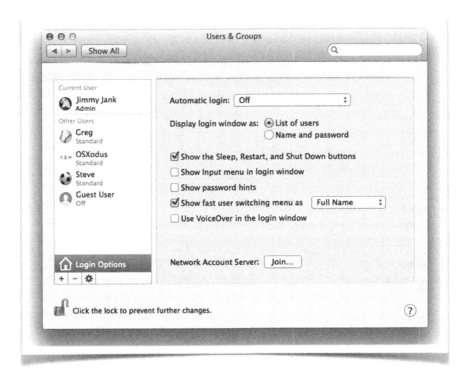

You see here on my test box that Automatic login is "off." I recommend you keep this off because auto-login can be a significant security risk. It's a far better practice to require a separate authentication process, particularly when remotely accessing resources.

Since Automatic login is off, the connection will fail and you'll just see a blank file list.

Note the "Share Screen…" and "Connect As…" buttons on the top right. Clicking either one will result in being prompted to log on, but they perform two very different functions.

I'm going to click "Connect As." Even though I'm logged in with the same user on both machines, I am still prompted to login.

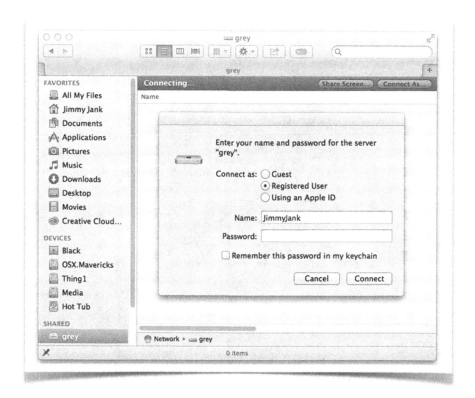

Once logged in, I'm immediately presented with all of the remote shares that, in this case, Jimmy Jank has access to. I am free to browse through these files as if they were any other local directory or share. And I can easily copy and paste files I want or directly edit them remotely. All of this is quite cool. The beauty here is that it is extremely easy while very secure. While you can indeed do this in Windows, it is an extremely involved process and requires a significant amount of technical expertise. In the past, I've made quite a bit of money getting paid to configure this very feature for people.

Now that we know how to directly access files on our remote system, let's try to use Back to My Mac's Screen Sharing functions, and discuss these features a bit more.

When I click "Share Screen," I'm prompted to logon. I'll again login as Jimmy Jank. If no one is logged on to the system currently, or if I'm logged on as Jimmy Jank on the remote host already, I'll be presented with the logon screen.

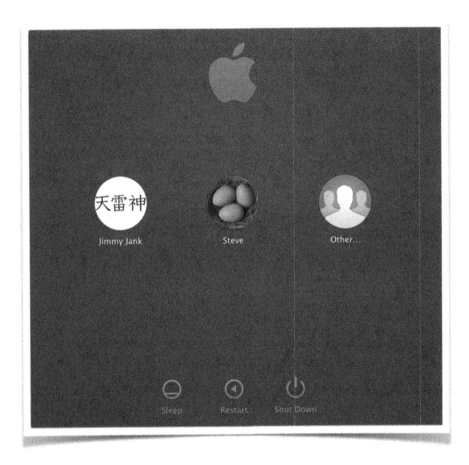

I'll login as Jimmy Jank, at which point I'll be given my full remote screen and work on the system as I please, as illustrated with the Remote Desktop functions described earlier.

This type of functionality obviously affords us a tremendous amount of flexibility. One such example would be accessing your home system from work in order to, say, bypass your company's firewall policies that may keep you from doing something you want to do. For instance, here in my office the firewall blocks all attempts of the folks here to go to Facebook. With Back to My Mac Screen Sharing, I can pop into my home system within seconds and check the status of my wall:

So, we can see how valuable Back to My Mac functionality is, how easy it is to set up, and how it's secure by default without us having to go through and configure a bunch of security settings.

But before we finish up, there are a couple of other cool things I want to talk about.

In the immediately preceding example, Jimmy Jank was logged on to the remote host "Grey." To review, Automatic login is off, so I'm still presented with the logon screen. When I logged on, I am presented with the session as Jimmy Jank.

But what if Steve was already logged onto Grey and doing something – checking mail or something? This is the cool part of Screen Sharing, and is a function of VNC.

If another user is already logged on to the host you are attempting to use Share Screen on, you are automatically presented with two options:

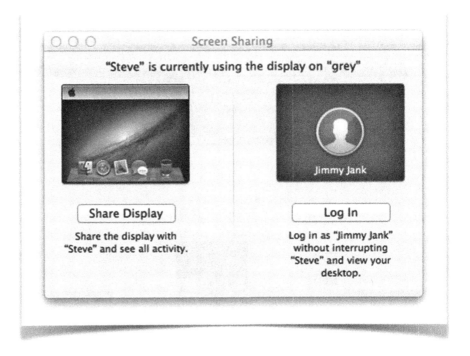

If I choose to (and have permission to), I can either share the screen with Steve and we can both work together, or I can initiate my own Screen Sharing session and work in my own user space. This is a built-in feature and doesn't require any configuration on your part.

In contrast to Windows 7 or 8, only one user can be logged on at a time via RDP. You've either got to logon to the user already logged on, or force the other user to log out. That's crappy functionality. You can certainly switch users if you are sitting in front of the machine, but not via RDP. Windows Server platforms allow you to have two simultaneous RDP sessions, but you'll pay hundreds of dollars to license the OS.

The last tidbit I wanted to cover is that Screen Sharing automatically supports multiple monitors. My host Grey has two monitors – one Apple HD Cinema display at 1920 × 1200, and another generic monitor at 1440 × 900.

My work rig has two 30" Apple Cinema Displays at 2560 × 1600, so I can actually use both monitors in my remote Screen Sharing session as if I were in front of the machine itself. This is a huge bonus for those of you with multiple monitors.

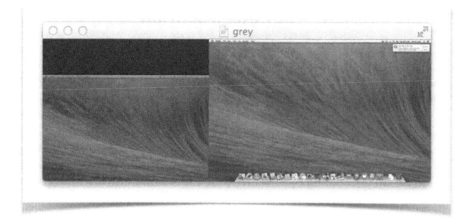

Of course, you may not want to use both monitors in your Screen Sharing session, which is no problem. In the Screen Sharing menu, you have full control over what monitors you wish to use along with other preferences for quality, etc.

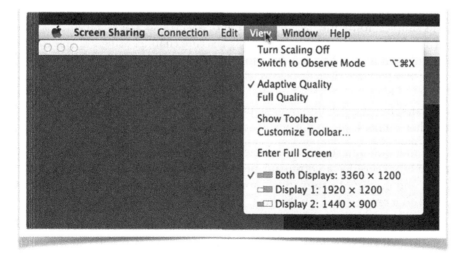

If you muck about with RDP settings in Windows 7, you can indeed use multiple monitors, but only if you purchased the Ultimate or Enterprise editions of the software. Yet another example of how Microsoft peddles cripple-ware to their users.

SSH SUPPLEMENT – ADVANCED SECTION

While Screen Sharing/VNC, Back to My Mac, and (as discussed in Chapter 5, OS X Server) WebDAV and VPN technologies for remote access are all powerful, secure ways to get to your data, OS X also supports what is called "Remote Logon." Remote Logon is just an OS X term for old-school "SSH." SSH stands for "Secure Shell" and is a technology that has been around for decades. Not many Windows users know about SSH (or if they do, they don't use it) and Microsoft often chooses to reinvent the wheel (sometime resulting in a "square") instead of implementing tried and true open-source technologies. To be fair, integrating open-source code into Windows gets a bit dicey in regard to licensing, but there are ways around that. Regardless, unless you go with third-party tools, there is no SSH in Windows.

This is a shame because SSH is a simple yet powerful and secure way of remotely accessing server resources. Some may find it a bit daunting, however, as it is a command-line utility without a graphical interface. That said, with just a bit of practice, you'll find that popping into an SSH shell (yes, that's redundant as is "PIN number") can be an extremely fast and effective way of getting things done.

In its simplest form, the overall operation of SSH consists of establishing a connection to the remote SSH host, creating a secure channel using PKI (please see the PKI section of Chapter 5 for more information), and then authenticating to the remote host over the secure channel. On a side note, SSH can be configured to both build the secure channel AND authenticate with public/private key pairs, but the default configuration for OS X is to build a secure channel and then authenticate to the host via a user-defined password.

Once the authentication is complete, the server "spawns" a bash shell (what you might consider a command prompt in Windows), and then pipes the input and output of commands through the SSH connection, thus presenting you with a remote shell on the host.

When you run the Terminal app on OS X, what you are doing is spawning a bash shell on your local computer. SSH would be as if you did the same thing on the host, except that you are on a remote client. While a more common usage of SSH is to simply get a command prompt on a remote host, the secure connection created via SSH can be used for any number of other purposes, including the secure exchange of data between applications (which must be able to use the SSH pipe); tunneling VNC connections through, in order to secure them; and even the establishment of a secure SOCKS proxy (as described in the advanced section of Chapter 1 on privacy).

However, in this section, we'll be establishing an SSH shell for the purpose of viewing the remote host's file structure, and then copying files from our client system to the remote host within the secure shell. Once you get proficient at this, you'll be able to easily and securely copy files between computers.

As previously stated, unlike Windows, OS X comes with the bits for both the SSH "server" and client applications.

OK – let's get started. The first thing we want to do is to make sure we've enabled "Remote Logon" in the "Sharing" preferences app. This is also where you'll specify which users can SSH into the host. By default, only the Administrators group can logon to the SSH server. Steve is just a Standard User on this box, so I had to add him to the access list. If you find that you have several users for whom you want to enable SSH access to the host, you might find it more easily maintained by creating an "SSH" group (you can call it whatever you would like, of course), and just maintaining the group membership; that way, you don't ever have to return to the Sharing applet to alter the access list.

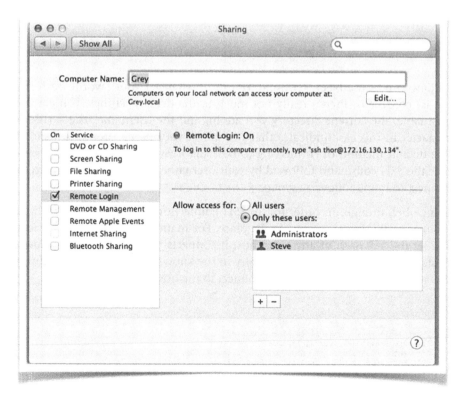

If we didn't add Steve to the access list, the behavior he would see on the client would be a bit counterintuitive. Rather than receiving a message that says "you don't have permission to log on" after putting in his password, he'd just be prompted for his password again. Now, you may be thinking "well, that's not really cool – it should tell us he doesn't have permission." But if you think about it within the context of security, the response is the proper one. If someone is trying to brute-force our SSH service to see if they can pop our server, giving them a message stating the user didn't have permission would at least let them know they got the password right. It would also validate that they chose a correct username. That's too much information for an attacker to have. In this case, even though we put in the right password, the system kept prompting for it because he didn't have permissions for the service. It's pretty smart, actually.

So let's see what happens here. Steve is going to fire up a Terminal session (the terminal.app) on the client "Black (like my heart)." Yes, that's really the name of the box.

```
O O O                        steve — bash — 80×24
Last login: Fri Sep 19 12:10:05 on console
black:~ steve$
```

As powerful as the bash (terminal, iTerm, or whatever your favorite bash client is) console is, there's really not much to the default settings. You get the hostname, the current directory you are in, and the username. The ~ (tilde) character in this case indicates that you are in your user's "home" directory. The default method of connecting to our SSH host is quite simple: you execute the SSH command followed by your username and the host you wish to connect to in the following syntax: `ssh steve@grey.local`. That's it!

Remember, though, in order for an SSH connection to be established, some manner of PKI exchange must take place. For matters of security, your client verifies the key hash of any given host it connects to against a list of known hosts. If the host doesn't have an entry in the known hosts file, it will prompt you to verify you actually want to connect to the host, as follows:

```
O O O                        steve — ssh — 80×24
Last login: Fri Sep 19 12:10:05 on console
black:~ steve$ ssh steve@grey.local
The authenticity of host 'grey.local (172.16.130.134)' can't be established.
RSA key fingerprint is 2c:31:7c:4e:6e:a4:b3:fa:fb:a0:0e:c0:e7:65:7e:41.
Are you sure you want to continue connecting (yes/no)? yes
```

Once we accept the connection, the RSA key signature will be added to the known hosts file. In this case, it's the first time Steve has ever initiated an SSH connection, so the known hosts file had to be created. What happens is that OS X creates a hidden directory in the user's home directory named .ssh (dot ssh). The "." initial character is what designates it as a hidden directory. The actual filename is known_hosts, and it is nothing but a text file. We can easily inspect its contents by using the "cd" command to change to our .ssh directory, and then using the cat command to view the contents of the file.

You'll notice that the "key" stored in the known_hosts file is not the same "key" shown when we first connected. That's because the "please verify" key is an actual hash of the public key while the contents of the known_hosts file is the public key itself. Again, this is a security measure. Rather than the remote host automatically giving you its public key upon connection, it will instead give you a hash of it. A hash is nothing more than a mathematical algorithm that results in a constant-length string no matter how big the input string is. In this case, the public key was hashed using an algorithm called "MD5" which creates a 128-bit result. By way of example, the MD5 hash for "You can't stop the signal Mal" is 3c:df:d1:f4:5a:46:10:4d:5b:5f:e3:2e:8b:1b:1d:43. That's the hex representation for the 128-bit result. In the same way, the MD5 hash for the entire script of *Serenity* (a movie by Joss Whedon) is c2:2a:29:0c:3c:83:38:32:92:b8:64:59:ef:32:c4:1e. So, no matter what length string (or binary data) you put into a MD5 hash function, you (theoretically) always get a unique 128-bit hash back. I caveat "theoretically" because there have been "collisions" with the MD5 hash where two different input strings resulted in the same hash. Anyway, when you connect to a host for the first time, you are presented with the MD5 hash of that host's public key.

In an environment where security is very important, you would have received the public key for that host before you connected. You would then either hash the public key to see if you get the same value presented to you by the host, or if you wanted to, you could edit the known_hosts file directly. In this way you prevent host "spoofing" where an attacker has hacked up your DNS server, or host file, or whatever necessary to make your machine think it's going to one host but is actually going to another.

Now that the host "grey" has its public key in the client user's known_hosts file, this data will be automatically verified, and you can SSH in without any further prompts.

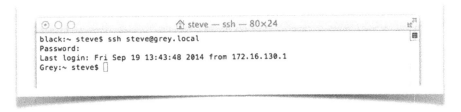

There we go. Steve has now established a secure, remote shell on the host Grey as evidenced by the prompt "Grey:~ steve$" Any commands entered here will be as if Steve were sitting at the host itself in a bash shell. It is a trivial, yet secure, way of establishing an almost immediate connect with the remote host. In fact, this is how I manage my Linux web server in Amazon Web Services. I simply SSH in, copy over updated files, and exit out. It's as simple as it can be, and it's fast.

Now, let's do a quick example of how to copy files over SSH. As you'll find when you keep digging deeper and deeper into OS X, the secure copy command, SCP, is also included in OS X by default. SCP (which stands for "secure copy") is both an SSH client and copy utility built into one. Meaning, you don't have to first establish an SSH shell to use it. SCP allows you to specify files you wish to copy to or from a host and, based on the syntax of the command, establish the connection, copy the files, and then terminate the connection.

Steve has created a document on the local system Black (like my heart) and wants to copy it over to the host Grey in his home directory. Using SCP, this can be done in a single command. Hopefully, this will give you a bit more insight into how powerful this type of access is, and how much time it can save you over establishing a Remote Desktop, navigating through Finder and copying files back and forth. The following screenshot shows a listing of Steve's Documents directory, the scp command, and a subsequent SSH into Grey to see if the file exists over there. This could be done with one simple SCP command, but I wanted to show you the progression of the example.

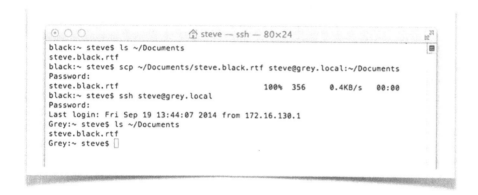

From terminal, all you would have to do in order to copy the file (or an entire directory if you wished) is type `scp  ~/Documents/steve.black.rtf steve@grey.local:~/Documents`.

This would specify to secure copy the source file ~/Documents/steve.black. rtf utilizing connection steve@grey.local and appending a ":" (colon) to then separate out the destination folder.

And that's that. There are, of course, a million other things you could do, such as remotely edit your web server configuration files, restart your mail server, create users, or anything else you can do from a command prompt.

Before we wrap up, I'm going to show you one more thing I've found very helpful.

To review, let's look at the default terminal bash session again where Steve has SSHed into Grey:

```
●  ○ ○                    ⌂ steve — ssh — 80×24
black:~ steve$ ssh steve@grey.local
Password:
Last login: Fri Sep 19 13:43:48 2014 from 172.16.130.1
Grey:~ steve$ ▯
```

In this case, you really need to carefully examine your bash prompt to see what host you are on, as it can be very easy to forget you are SSHed into a different host. You may find yourself (as I have before) trying to do something on one host when you are actually on a different one. In order to help us more readily identify what host we are on, we're going to leverage what is called the .profile file, which is simply a text file that contains specific information regarding options you wish to have present in your bash session. This can include environmental variables, aliases, and, of course, options for your bash prompt. We'll choose the latter in order to ensure we are aware (or help anyway) that we are on a different host.

There are other files that allow us to specify bash options, but .profile is "sourced" or executed each time you logon, even via SSH. What I'm going to do is create a .profile file that contains specific prompt data and store it in my home (~) directory on Grey. In this way, when I SSH into Grey, I'll get a special prompt. While you can do many things in .profile, I'll just specify some parameters for colors, a cool graphic, and my prompt data. Here's the text I'll use for my .profile.

```
tput sgr0
PURPLE= $(tput setaf 5)
BLUE= $(tput setaf 4)
GREEN= $(tput setaf 2)
RED= $(tput setaf 1)
GRAY= $(tput setaf 7)
BOLD= $(tput bold)
RESET= $(tput sgr0)
```

```
export PURPLE
export BLUE
export GREEN
export RED
export GRAY
export BOLD
export RESET

export CLICOLOR= 1
export GREP_OPTIONS= '--color= auto'

export PS1= "💀\[${RED}\] \u \[${BOLD}${GRAY}\]on: \[$BLUE\]\h
\[$GRAY\]: \@ \ncurrent: \[$PURPLE\]\w\[$GRAY\]\n☞ \[$RESET\]"

export LSCOLORS= GxFxCxDxBxegedabagaced
#export LSCOLORS= GxFxCxDxBxhxhxhxhxcxcx

export PS2= "continue ->"
```

The first thing you may notice is that I've got a couple of cool little icons embedded in my .profile file. This is a great feature of bash and OS X in general. It's not possible to do this in a Windows command prompt, but with OS X, there are a couple of ways you can embed your own icons into text-based files.

The easiest way is to just copy and paste icons from the OS X "Special Characters" collection. If you run something like Text Editor, you can go to the Edit menu and select "Special Characters" at the bottom. You'll see a collection of many different icon-based graphics. Simply choose the one you want, copy it from the Text Editor, and paste it into your .profile file. It's as simple as that.

You can do this within any compliant application, including third-party apps. For instance, I'm going to fire up my favorite editor, BBEdit. It of course includes the Special Characters option.

Selecting "Special Characters" pulls up a collection of various icons grouped into different categories. As you can see, I chose a cool little skull to spice up my prompt.

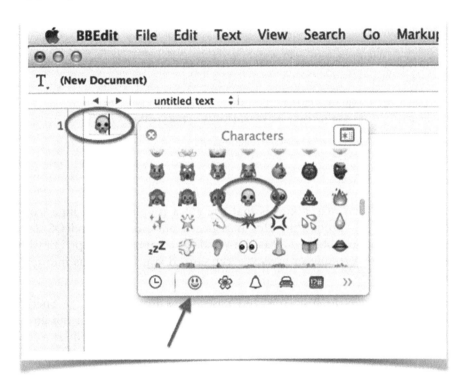

Just select the icon/character you want and it shows up in your document. Now copy the character and paste it into your .profile file while editing it in nano. Wa-la!

I've got the emoji group selected, but you can move through whatever group you like and select your favorite characters.

Continuing on, this file needs to be saved in Steve's home directory on Grey. I could easily go to the Grey host and paste it into a .profile file, but let's create this file through an SSH shell using the "nano" text editor, also installed by default.

To follow along with the following screenshot, I'm going to copy the contents of this file to my local buffer on Black (like my heart) as the user Steve, SSH into Grey, run "nano," paste the contents into nano, and save the text as .profile. I'll then exit the SSH shell and reestablish it. Let's see what happens – remember, we've first copied the text from either a file, email, or whatever.

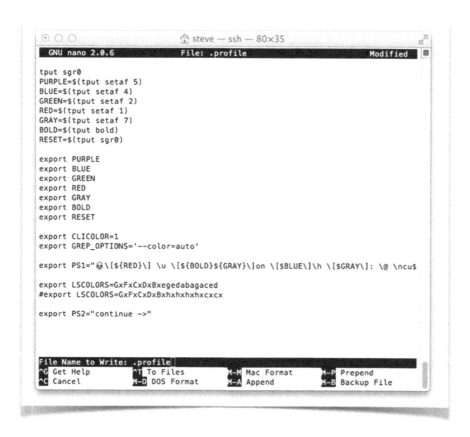

1. SSH into Grey and run nano (a shell text editor), passing along the filename .profile

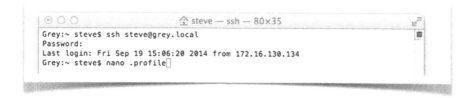

2. Inside the nano editor, I COMMAND+V to paste the text into the editor. Once in, I CONTROL+O to write the file out (note how .profile automatically appears in the filename box). Once written, I CONTROL+X to exit out.

3. When we exit nano, we are returned to the bash prompt on Grey. We'll exit, thus returning to our own terminal prompt on Black, and then reconnect via SSH:

Since the .profile file now exists in Steve's home directory on the host Grey, that file is sourced upon logon via SSH, parsed, and the prompt options we selected implemented in bash. We now see a cool skull icon, the username in red, the word "on" in grey, and the hostname. On a separate line we see the current directory indicated by "current:" and the tilde. Then on another line we see a little hand with the finger pointing at the actual prompt.

Now there's no mistaking the fact that I'm on the Grey host. To be sure, I implement a similar .profile on my own system, but they differ enough so that I can still immediately tell that I'm SSHed into a different box.

And with that, we'll end the Remote Access chapter.

CHAPTER 5

OS X Server

When it comes to politics, I've never been a fan of campaigns where the primary impetus was rooted in telling the voters how bad the other guy is. If you want to win my vote, tell me about who you are, what you think, and what you plan to do – don't tell me about how the other guy is a schmuck for spending too much money on this, or for voting for that. It may help me with what choice *not* to make, but it doesn't give me the real information I need.

That said, it's always fun to have at least a little mud-slinging, so here I go.

When it comes to server products, Microsoft has done a good job in providing solid platforms from which to build and provide internet services. But this comes at a significant cost to any entity who decides to deploy Windows-based services. This is not just in what can be extremely expensive licensing, but also in areas such as support (both from Microsoft and third-party providers), and from "hidden" costs such as having to pay someone like me (a lot in some cases) to come in and secure your installations. The overhead of operating a Windows environment is also nontrivial. Patch management alone can be an extremely difficult thing to properly handle, and I can tell you from first-hand experience that, in the largest Microsoft production environments in the world, even Microsoft doesn't know how to do it.

Now, I don't expect you to require a massive server farm in order to provide services you want to make available, but I do suspect that once you read about what you can do with OS X Server you'll be ready to dive in and become a server admin. Well, maybe. You'll have the opportunity, anyway.

Microsoft used to provide for small business with the Small Business Server (SBS) product, but then just decided to sunset the software. Many, many small businesses, and even home users, used this suite of products to run their own mail, web, and file services. But then Microsoft pulled the rug out from under these people when they figured they couldn't make enough money selling the product. They'll pay 6.4 billion dollars for an ad delivery company, only to write off 6 billion in losses a few years later, and they'll spend 5 billion in one quarter on payola for vendors to schlep Azure services, but they'll abandon customers that actually use their products without a care

CONTENTS

Medium Level Tech ... 161
*Here's what we'll do
in the medium section 161*

Advanced Level
Tech 180
*Here's what we'll do
in the advanced section 180*
*Starting and Configuration
of Mail 181*
Introducing PKI 184
The Conversation 184
The Math 187
Deeper Explanation 188
Postfix Mail Services..........192
*Using Certificates to
Secure Services 192*

if they lose a few bucks. And in actuality, SBS made money; but I guess it just wasn't enough. Go figure.

Let's do a comparison. Let's say you want to provide server-based mail, calendar, and contact management to your customers, or even just you and your family. The Microsoft solution for this is of course Exchange. Unfortunately, you just can't buy "Exchange" as a product and use it. You must purchase Windows Server with multiple licenses; if you are going to follow the "best practices" model, you'll actually have to purchase Windows Server for multiple systems, as one needs two domain controls at a minimum. Once you've done that, you must prepare your Active Directory forest, then the AD domain, and you must install and configure several ancillary services you most likely don't need, but that Exchange must have in place to even be installed. You then need to master PowerShell if you want to perform any level of administration. It's no wonder that Microsoft has "meditation rooms" in every office. Seriously.

In addition, if we want to provide web pages for visitors, we have to buy Windows Server Web Edition and go through the rigamarole of configuring IIS (Internet Information Services).

With the single purchase of OS X Server, you get all of the following services: Web, Wiki (which you don't even get with MSFT products), Mail, Calendar, Instant Messaging, Contacts, centralized Time Machine backups, Profile Manager Server to automatically configure your iOS devices, Open Directory Services, File Sharing, VPN, an Internet Caching Service, DHCP, DNS, FTP, a NetInstall service and an automatic Software Update Service to deploy updates automatically within your organization.

This full-featured suite of server products does come at a cost though: $19.99. Nope, I didn't mess up the decimal point. Nineteen dollars and ninety-nine cents. And these are not some Micky Mouse little apps that Apple threw together. These are enterprise-based, robust, stable products used by the largest companies in the world such as Google, Apple, IBM, AT&T, and technical companies planet-wide. These are customized versions of Apache for web services, Postfix for SMTP, Dovecot for IMAP and POP3, and BIND for DNS.

Now it depends on where you go and exactly what you buy, but for less than the price of a *single user license* of Windows Server Standard 2012, you can buy a Mac-Mini preloaded with OS X Server along with a 3-year hardware warranty and 3 years of Enterprise Support. And you can have as many users as you want using as many services as you want, as long as you want to. And you can run it on as many processors as you want to, without additional licensing costs. That's something to think about.

OK, enough jibba-jabba. Let's get into how to get rolling with OS X Server.

MEDIUM LEVEL TECH

Here's what we'll do in the medium section

Start and configure web services
Start and configure Wiki
Logon and configure Blog
Post documents to our Wiki.

In this section, we'll go through setting up just a few of the services I think you'll want to use right off the bat. We'll be doing this all through the Server App, so you won't even have to drop down to iTerm to do any configuration work – that's for the Advanced Section (and we're going to have a BLAST!).

The first thing we'll do is download OS X Server (in this example it is the Mavericks version) and install it. Once the app is installed, you simply run the server app and you're ready to configure all of your services. It is literally that easy. Oh, and all of the services are secure by default. Again, as enterprise-based, open source, tried and true internet services, all the settings are secured from outside access from the moment you install them. Installation is trivial; simply run the Server app once downloaded and it does the rest, showing you its progress along the way.

When you open the Server App you'll be asked to connect to a server instance. The user context you are logged on as is different from the server context – that's why you logon to the server service via the app. If you have multiple servers, you can manage them all from this one app.

After installation, your first launch of Server gives you a Getting Started screen where you can explore help for various subjects.

We'll close out and connect to our newly created server instance.

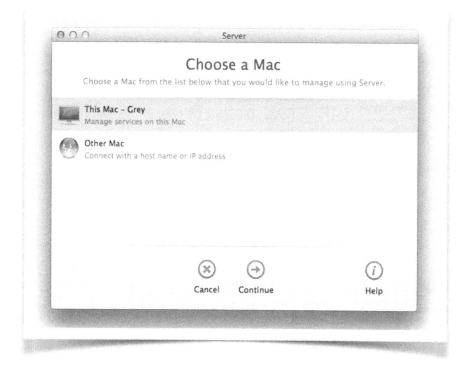

Here's what you'll see when you open the Server App.

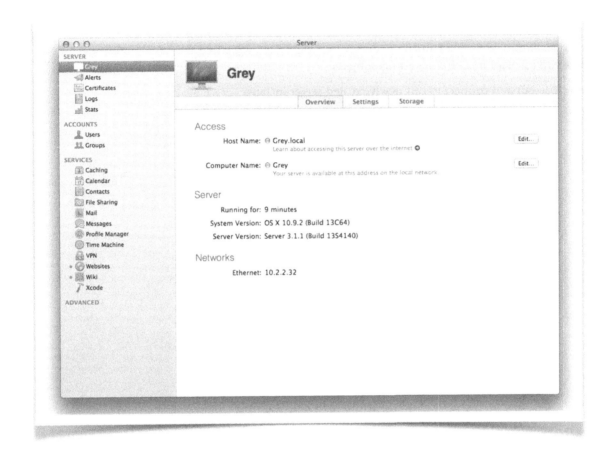

Just to let you know how easy it is to get started and actually DO something, click on Websites and turn them on (with the slider). The App will actually launch Apache for you with a default configuration. Once started, you'll see the little green light and Server App will tell you that services are already available on your local network at ServerName.local. In my case, my server name is "Grey." I name all my servers by color now. I'm not sure why, but I got tired of naming them things like Vor, Sif, Magni, and other "Thor" idiom-like names. For whatever reason, I can associate color with services in my head better than a name.

Now, let's click on Wiki under Services in the left pane and turn the Wiki on. Once started, you'll also see that the service is available on your local network.

With IIS (Microsoft's Internet Information Server web service) once you go through and install all the components (a daunting task in itself) you get an IIS welcome page. That's it. If you want to actually do something, you have to download and configure whatever it is you want to do.

Note that you don't actually have to have the Web service running to use the Wiki – however, if you don't then you won't get this nifty navigation page when you go to the root of the site. You'd have to navigate to servername. local/Wiki to get to the Wiki folder. You'll most likely want the web service running anyway, but I wanted to make sure you were aware the Wiki is not dependent upon the Web service.

Just by turning on these two services, you are already ready for whatever users you've created to log on and create their own Wiki pages, create and manage profiles, and manage subscriptions to other people's Wiki pages. Apple is like that – they don't just give you a service, they make it so you can immediately begin work doing the things you want to do.

If you open up a browser on a system on your network (or on the server itself) and navigate to ServerName.local, you'll immediately see the options you have available.

This will verify that your services are up and running. Before moving on, now would be a good time to bring up the fact that in order to log on to the Wiki service (or any other services) you'll need a user account. You will have already created your admin account, but you might now want to create other user accounts for use with the Wiki.

While you could certainly use your admin account to create and manage your Wiki documents and Blog, you should create a separate, nonadministrative (called "standard") user for this purpose. It's always a good idea to run as a standard user rather than an admin, even on OS X.

You can create users now or go back and do it later, but you will need at least one account to logon with. Let's quickly run through creating a standard user. I'm going to create a Wiki user called OSXodus that I'll use in further examples. From the dock, select the System Preferences icon and then select Users and Groups . Note this needs to be done on the server, as that is where the actual logon process occurs when users logon to the web or Wiki service. Click the "lock" to allow changes and create a standard user as I have:

With my OSXodus user created, I can now logon to the Wiki as that user. I've actually gone ahead and created user accounts for my ace bones Steve and Greg. If you picked up a copy of Thor's Microsoft Security Bible previously, then you'll know all about Steve and Greg. If not, Steve is a Scot living in Bermuda where he runs his own ISP, and Greg is a convict living in an Australian penal colony. You'll find out all you'll ever want to know about them in the pages that follow.

Now, the thing with creating local user accounts is that, by default, they show up on your Logon screen when you've locked your screen or restarted the server. In my case, after creating my users, I'll see this:

I obviously don't want this, as these guys are only going to be logging on to my Wiki service externally and they'll never logon directly to my server. So what I'll do is hide these users so I don't have to look at them every time I go to logon.

There are several ways of doing this, but I'll show you an easy way to do this by using the "defaults write" directive in terminal. We'll cover terminal more in the advanced section of this chapter, but since we're talking about Users, it's appropriate to show you this now. Simply fire up iTerm or Terminal and type this at your bash prompt:

```
sudo defaults write /Library/Preferences/com.apple.loginwindow
HiddenUsersList -array-add osxodus steve greg
```

This will add the users to the "com.apple.loginwindow.plist" file so that they'll be hidden automatically the next time we go to logon:

Note that the syntax for the usernames is case sensitive. When I first starting working with OS X Server, I mistakenly used the actual "name" of my users to hide, as opposed to the "user account." As such, using initial capital letters as in "array-add Steve Greg OSXodus" would not work.

OK, let's get back to our configuration.

As previously stated, OS X Server offers substantial features right out of the box. In addition to Wiki and Blog functionality, the Wiki/Web service also allows you to store and manage your own documents to share with others or simply keep as a distribution point for yourself.

iCloud is a great service, and I use it myself, but there are going to be instances where you simply don't want to put personal information out into a cloud service. This is where your Wiki Document Management comes into play.

Though everything we'll do in this section is via the Wiki service, we'll discuss three separate (but related) features: "My Documents," "Wiki," and "Blog."

While all similar, these features differ mainly in the areas of permissions and access. "My Documents," as you'll see, is more of a "private" repository for whatever files you wish to put on the server. The files you store in My Documents are accessible via the web, and you can set permissions to share files to other users if if you wish. The thing to remember about "My Documents" files is that you can't access them via WebDAV. I'll get into what WebDAV is in a moment, but for now just remember that when we discuss accessing files from your iPhone or iPad via WebDAV, your "My Documents" files won't be accessible.

That is a perfect segue into the use of Wikis, which is where you will be able to create Wikis and store files for collaboration with others. As with My Documents, different users can set different permissions on individual Wiki items. The big difference is that the documents within your Wiki are indeed accessible from applications supporting WebDAV. Finally, you have the Blog, which is quite similar to the Wiki, other than the fact that you set permissions for your Blog at the actual Blog level. Inside of the Blog you can't set individual permissions on Blog entries.

When you logon to your Wiki/web service, you're taken to your "main" page. At the top right, you'll see all of your edit, settings, and service options. One of these is "Documents." This is where we'll upload a file to make available via a web browser, as well as via your iPhone or iPad.

It's time to logon and get things done. Using the "Log in to access more services" option in the top left, I'll be logging on as my OSXodus user and uploading files to "My Documents." Once logged on I'll select "Documents" from the menu in the top left.

With the Documents option selected, we'll click the "+" sign and select "Upload file to 'OSXodus'…" An "Upload File" dialog is presented where you can navigate to a file and select it for upload.

In my case, I've created and selected a "HelloWorld.pages" file from my Documents folder. I've purposefully chosen a Pages document because of the way Pages stores documents. While the file shows up on my system as "HelloWorld.pages," it is actually a zipped (compressed) document containing other files. When I select and upload "HelloWorld.pages," the Wiki will display the file as "HelloWorld.pages.zip." I bring this up because it may cause you some trouble when you upload documents depending upon what browser you use to do so. Safari will see the "HelloWorld.pages" document as a single file, and when you select it from the Upload dialog box, you'll see the "Choose" option is available:

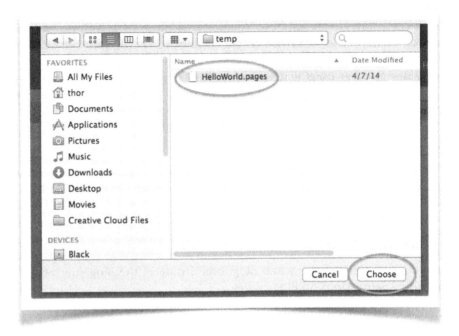

However, if you are using Firefox to upload, in the process of selecting the file Firefox will "think for you" and assume that if you select a compressed file that you want to display the contents of the file to subsequently upload:

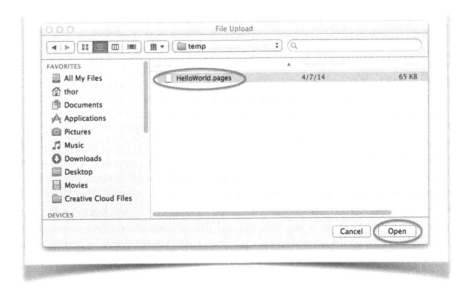

The Firefox dialog option is "Open," and not "Choose" as it is in Safari. If you select "Open," it won't select the file for upload; rather, it will display the contents of the zipped file:

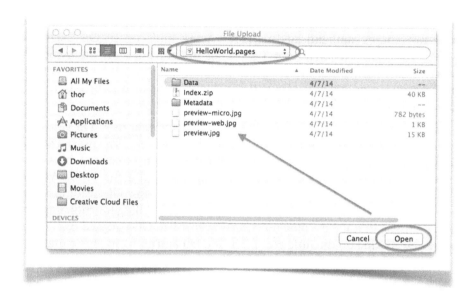

I do not know of a work-around for this. Even if you change the file extension the Firefox dialog will still show the contents of the file. I had to use Safari to upload all of the .pages files used as examples in this chapter.

With the file uploaded, it is now visible in the list of My Documents.

You may now log on from any web browser and retrieve the file. Easy-peasy.

We should now talk about permissions, and do so by expanding the scope of our example out to include Greg and Steve. As things sit right now, the OSXodus user is the only one to have posted documents. The default permissions on the HelloWorld.pages.zip file in OSXodus' "My Documents" folder have two entries: authenticated users-No Access and Logged On Users-No Access. As such, the only user (including unauthenticated "anonymous" users connecting to the Wiki) who will see anything in My Documents is the OSXodus user. No one else will see this document; it is private to the OSXodus user.

Let's now engage in actions more indicative of a normal user. I'm going to pretend I'm Steve, and I'm going to enable Blog functionality, customize my settings, create a Wiki, and then post a document that I'll share with Greg. First, as Steve would do, I'll go get a blow-up doll and a cup of tea. When I logon for the first time I'm going to do a few things: I'll customize my account, changing my Icon, Profile colors, and enabling Blog functionality. By default, users do not have Blog functionality enabled. Once logged on, I'll do all this by clicking on the little gear in the top left and going to My Settings.

It's all pretty self explanatory from here. Once you enable the Blog feature you'll immediately see the Blog option and be able to Blog till your heart's content. I went ahead and customized my icon and such by selecting "Appearance" on the left.

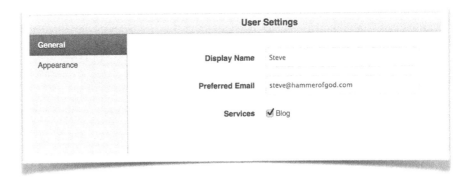

With the look and feel I want, I'm going to click the "+" (plus sign) icon and create a Wiki called, you guessed it, "Steve's Wiki." Once created, I'll click the gear again and this time select "Wiki Settings."

This is where we're going to set permissions for the Wiki. By default, there are two user "contexts": "All logged in users" and "All unauthenticated users." Each has "No access" defined, which means that Steve is currently the only one who can read and write to the Wiki. We're going to change that so that any logged-on user can view the Wiki with Read Only permissions.

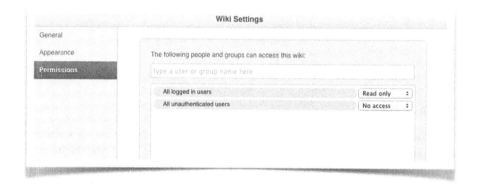

There are "comments" settings in this pane as well, but we'll talk about that in a bit. These permissions will prevent any anonymous (anyone not logged in) users from even seeing that Steve has a Wiki at all.

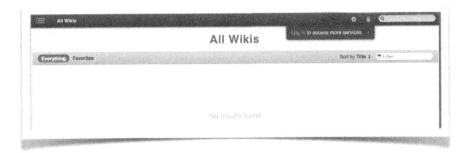

An unauthenticated user can navigate to "All Wikis" but they won't see anything. Well, they won't see Steve's Wiki – if other Wikis have been defined that have permissions other than "No Access" set for "All unauthenticated users" then those Wikis will be visible here. Let's get Greg to logon, though, and see what he sees:

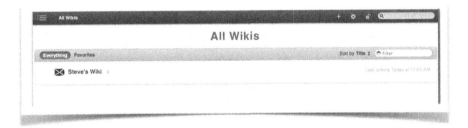

There it is, Steve's Wiki.

We're not limited to just the two default permissions, of course. If I choose to (as Steve), I can add Greg as a specific user who has Read and Write permissions to my Wiki. Going back to my Wiki Settings and the Permissions pane, I'll simply type in Greg's name to add an access list for him. As I type, the Wiki settings will automatically populate a drop-down menu with the Username and Account Name of users matching the text as I type it.

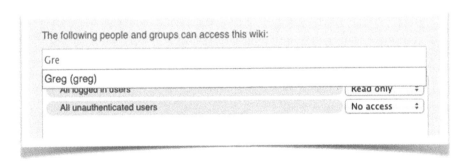

I'll select "Greg (greg)" and give him "Read & write."

Now when Greg logs in, he'll be able to edit Wiki data and post documents. Of course, being a convict we probably don't want to let him do that, but Steve's crazy like that.

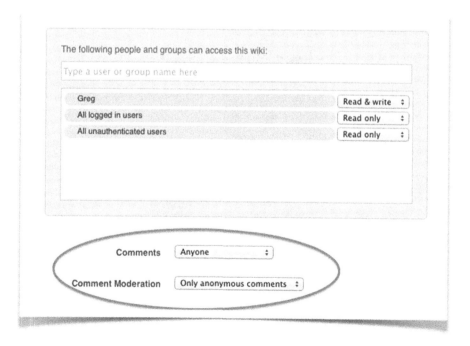

So, as you can see, we have a great deal of flexibility as to what users can see, access, or change on an account-by-account basis. Finally, let's review the "Comments" options also viewed in the Permissions tab. I'm now going to give everyone (anonymous users) access to read Steve's Wiki and allow people to leave comments. However, not "trusting" anonymous users, I'm going to set my Moderation settings to where I must approve posted comments from anonymous users while allowing logged-on users (people with accounts) to be able to post with immediate approval.

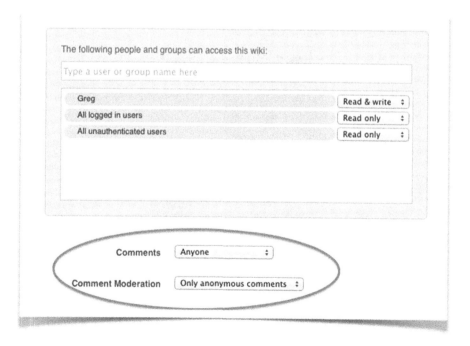

Permissions set for individual files in My Documents works the same way. You can set which users you wish to have access to files on a user-by-user basis. But again, "My Documents" are only available via a web browser.

But let's extend this file-access functionality out to our mobile iDevices. Going back into our Server App, let's select the Wiki configuration and enable the "Enable WebDAV access to Wiki files" checkbox.

WebDAV stands for Web Distributed Authoring and Versioning, and is an HTTP standard designed for online collaboration and management of documents via the web. All of the Apple mobile productivity applications (collectively called iWork) support WebDAV, which means you can manage documents in Pages, Numbers, Keynote and other applications directly from your mobile device.

With WebDAV enabled, we can now very easily access our private documents from anywhere.

Here I'm going to open Pages on my iPhone, logon to my Wiki service, and retrieve a copy of a HelloWorld file I posted in a Wiki I created called "OSXodus" for editing.

I don't have any documents on my iPhone, so you only see the "Create New" option. If I had local copies of documents they would be populated in this screen (which you will see shortly).

In order to retrieve a document via WebDAV, I'm going to click on the upper left "+" sign as indicated here:

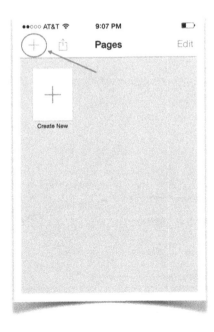

Clicking the plus sign displays the following options: "Create Document," "Copy from iTunes," and "Copy from WebDAV." If the "Copy from iTunes" option seems odd, it's only because iTunes can be used to manage shared documents from your iPhone and computer as well. It's not as if you're going to open up Pink Floyd, Comfortably Numb on your phone or anything. We're going to select "Copy from WebDAV," of course.

We are then presented with a logon screen – in my case, I'm logging on to Grey.local over HTTPS. By default, your Mac OS X Server configuration will have created a self-signed certificate for use with HTTPS. None of your client devices will trust this certificate by default, so you will be presented with a warning that the certificate could not be verified. You can go ahead and accept the cert and you'll then be presented with the logon window.

Upon logon, you'll see a list of all of the Wikis you have permissions to access, and you can drill down through the Wikis to get the document you want. Our "HelloWorld.pages.zip" file is under Wikis -> OSXodus as shown in the cascaded iPhone screen shots:

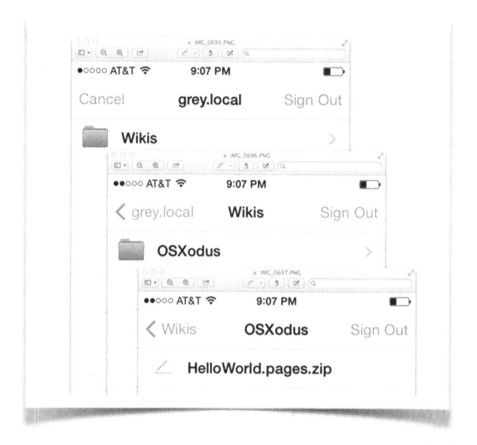

Once we select "HelloWorld.pages.zip," the file is downloaded, unzipped, and stored on our phone locally:

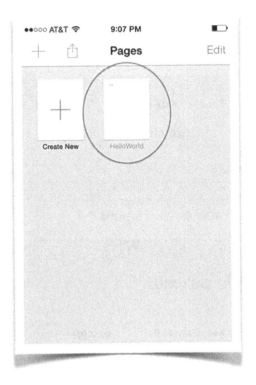

And there you have it!

ADVANCED LEVEL TECH

Here's what we'll do in the advanced section

Creating and using Self-Signed Certificates
Creating host CSR via Server App interface and parsing CA-Issued Certificates into certificate store (Keyring Access)
Creating Wildcard CSR via OpenSSL in bash, moving approriate key, cert, and chain files into /etc/certificates, assigning permissions, and editing .conf files to use customized certificate (can't be done in Server App as it won't allow "" character)*
Configure Mail (Postfix, Dovecot) to use wildcard certificate
Configure Sieve scripts for customized server-based rule parsing and access.

Starting and Configuration of Mail

Mail functionality in OS X Server is provided by a number of different sub-services. SMTP services are provided by Postfix and IMAP/POP mailbox functionality (where the mail you receive is processed) is handled by Dovecot. Pigeonhole/Sieve is implemented within the Dovecot framework and allows for extremely granular mail filtering and processing. We'll get into some really cool examples of that later in the chapter. In addition to standard mail services, OS X Server also includes built-in anti-virus and email blacklist and greylist features.

Though you've got multiple applications supporting mail, all you have to do in order to launch them is to start up your Mail services in Server App. When you do this for the first time, many features are automatically installed and configured. The first thing you'll notice is that OS X Server Mail (herein collectively referred to as "Mail") immediately begins downloading update virus definitions upon start.

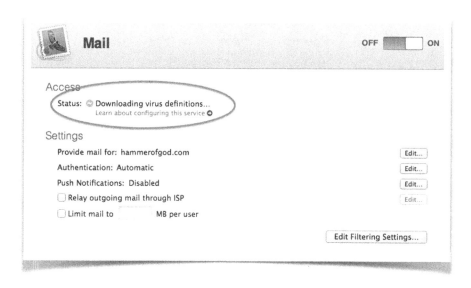

Once the download is complete and services started, you can see what additional Filtering Settings you've got available.

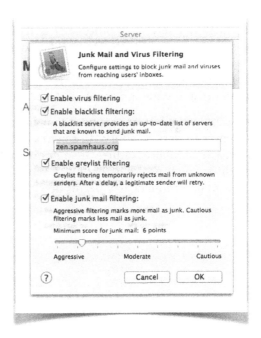

Enabling virus filtering enables ClamAV (ClamXav to be specific) and ensures all inbound emails will be scanned for viruses before being delivered to your inboxes. Blacklist filtering will require the incoming IP address of the sending SMTP engine be compared against a constantly updated database of "bad" email SPAM, virus, and other sketchy types. If the IP address of the sender is listed, Postfix will immediately reject the connection.

"Greylisting" is an interesting feature, which I actually use in all my email server implementations. Basically, what greylisting does is tell a sending SMTP server that the mail service is temporarily unavailable and to try again. SMTP servers that follow RFC 6647 (Email Greylisting) will obediently wait a bit and try to send the message again. Greylisting connection attempts are tracked and the next time (normally very soon) the server tries to deliver your message, it will be allowed in. The reason this works well to combat spam is that none of the client-side, virus-based or mass mailing scanners out there implement "resend if busy" functionality and will never try to resend you spam or abusive mail again.

The "junk mail" filtering is a service that examines the contents on inbound mail for tell-tale signs of spam. This is based on a match-list of specific terms and other characteristics of spam. This service won't block the emails, but rather it simply marks the header with the text *** JUNK MAIL *** so you can have client-side filtering rules do whatever you want them to do.

You will, of course, have to configure the DNS zone for your domain to have its MX records point to the external IP address of your router, which you presumably have forwarding SMTP to your OS X Server.

This next section will do a deep-dive into how to secure your mail services with certificates so that you can protect mail in transit as well as secure remote logon to SMTP and IMAP service. Oh, and POP as well, if you still want to use that noise.

When we first accessed our newly started Web/Wiki services via HTTPS, this was done using the default, automatically created "self-signed" certificate generated when the server is installed. Before getting into the processes around managing certificates in OS X Server, let's talk a bit about certificates in themselves.

There's a lot of mystery surrounding certificates, what they do, and how they are created. Many companies such as Verisign or GoDaddy want you to believe that certificates are some kind of "magic security device" and, as such, they think you should pay hundreds of dollars for one. First off, understand that a certificate is nothing more than a collector/object that stores RSA encryption key data. There's no magic there at all, unless you consider big prime numbers some manner of sorcery. Let's explore that a bit, shall we?

Anytime someone tries to simplify something very complex, by the nature of the goal, certain elements will have to be merged into easier-to-handle components. By way of example, if I wish to describe the purpose, usage, and control considerations while operating a bicycle, I wouldn't bother with describing how ball-bearings work, how the chain is constructed, or how I stole one from my friend Leon when I was 13. There are also some things that just can't be explained until one learns it oneself. Consistent with the bicycle analogy, consider "balance." I can tell you what it is, what it does, and what happens when you don't have it, but you'll never really know until you bust your ass a few times, and figure it out on your own.

The following overview is something like the bicycle analogy – there will be simplification, but you'll hopefully end up understanding things much better. I'll break it down into little pieces, but let me iterate, these examples are generalized. I'm verbose in sections so as to make sure there is no room for error. So, when I repeat myself a couple of times you'll know why.

Introducing PKI

While not specifically related to OS X, given the importance of security and encryption, I think a PKI primer is appropriate. PKI stands for "Public Key Infrastructure." Here's what that means, by way of another analogy:

As it relates to encryption, it can almost always be thought of in the terms of a "conversation" two parties want to have in private. So private, in fact, no one should ever, ever, ever be able to figure out what was said during that conversation – even if it was recorded. How long that "ever, ever, ever" is depends on how strong the encryption is. For the purposes of this article, let's assume it is long enough not to matter – meaning, time-bound entropy has rendered the data's value null. That's a nice way of saying "by the time it's cracked, it will have turned into thermodynamic poo." Now, the "two" entities can actually be any number of people exchanging data, or even encryption for one's self. I'm sure there are quite a few of you who cipher your own bits all the time.

The Conversation

Here's a "for instance": As some of you may know, the "players" in PKI examples are always "Bob" and "Alice." They are the quintessential couple we regard insofar as encrypted conversations are concerned. I, however, will not perpetuate this precedent. Why? Because Bob and Alice are obviously up to something sketchy, or they wouldn't always be the ones we talk about. I'm not sure if they're doing that spouse-swapping thing, or planning an attack against the International House of Pancakes, but I'm not supporting it. One shudders. So we'll make this personal, between you and me, because I know you trust me.

So, I want to send you an encrypted message in the mail. If I encrypt the letter and mail it to you, no one will ever know what the contents are. That includes *you* until I can somehow get you the passcode to decrypt it. Somehow, I need to get you this decryption code, or "key," as the case may be, so you'll have what you need to decrypt my message. Though an infinitely simplified example, it's similar to having to know what number (key) to use on your Captain Crunch Decoder Ring to decode "S.S. Guppy." The overall PKI structure is a way I can *get you the secret key* so you can decrypt the message I sent you. More importantly, it's a way of doing so in a way that no one can eavesdrop and steal it. To be precise, they can eavesdrop, they just won't be able to understand the observed data, and it will be useless to them.

So, let's say I want to call and give you the password that decrypts the encrypted letter, but we both know the NSA is listening to our calls in addition to reading our mail (which they actually are). It's important to understand that even the strongest PKI encryption won't help if the actual letter is encrypted with a passcode like "dog", or something else with a small keyspace. The "keyspace" is the smallest unit of possible characters (or binary data) required to comprise the passcode. If we were only allowed a single, lowercase character as our passphrase/password, then the "keyspace" would be the letters a–z; the keyspace would be 26 characters. If we could only use a single character but it could be uppercase and lowercase, then the keyspace would be the letters a–z and A–Z. The keyspace here would be 52 characters.

The smaller the keyspace, the easier to crack. For purposes of this example, we'll consider "keyspace" synonymous with "length," with the caveat that keyspace "strength" is also dependent upon the character set used. The more characters one can use as a base for the keyspace, the better. For example, using all lowercase characters results in a smaller, less secure keyspace than using uppercase and lowercase letters with numbers.

To illustrate how "length" directly impacts the keyspace, consider now that we can use up to a 2-character passphrase which consists of upper and lowercase letters. We can now have a passphrase of "a" to "z" and "A" to "Z" and then something like "aZ" or of course "Ff." The upper and lowercase allowance again gives us a "base" of 52 characters. But now that we can have two characters we have to do a bit of math to figure out the keyspace. We know that a single a–Z passphrase has a 52-character keyspace. Adding the second character exponentially increases the keyspace, such that you would square the base – in this case 52^2 or 2,704. Since we can have a 1- or 2-character passphrase, to find the keyspace we will add the 1-character keyspace of 52 with the 2-character keyspace of 52^2 resulting in a total keyspace of 2,756. So you can see how adding just one character greatly increases the keyspace. The longer, the better. If you are invested in how to further calculate the keyspace, you just take the exponent of the character length such as this for a 5-character passphrase: $baseline + baseline^2 + baseline^3 + baseline^4 + baseline^5$. I'll save you the trouble and tell you this yields a keyspace of 387,659,012.

So, when I initially encrypt the letter, I'm going to use a long password with a large keyspace, so I won't be worried about the NSA seeing it as it goes by. Nor will I worry if they "record" (keep) the encrypted data in order to attempt to decode it as time goes on. That part's easy – I simply use a strong key to encrypt the data. But as I said, somehow I have to get the letter's password itself to you so you can open (decrypt) it. That's the tricky part. How do we do that with the NSA listening? Well, in today's world, I could just FedEx it to you because they are too busy being clever and watching Facebook and Twitter to remember that people can still send parcel packages. But let's get back to our example. For the sake of argument, let's say the password to decrypt the letter itself is `Shamma_Lamma&&Ding!$Dong`. Here's how we are going to exchange it:

PKI is a function where a person, entity, or process makes two keys. One is a public key which anyone can have, and the other is a private key which only the *owner* has. The "ownership" of the keys is all procedural; this means that anyone who gains physical access to the keys can access encrypted data. There's no "mathematical" characteristic that denotes ownership otherwise. As it relates to PKI, and more specifically what I will describe shortly as RSA, when data is being encrypted it is always with a public key of some sort. Public keys only encrypt – they never decrypt. In kind, private keys are only used to decrypt data. They never encrypt. Since this is the advanced chapter, you may know all or some of this. But you still may be thinking, "Why is it one can securely share the public key?" This is, of course, the basis of PKI encryption.

A common mistake people make regarding encryption is they think public and private keys are used to encrypt the entire contents of "the letter" and then subsequently decrypt the contents of the letter. This is not true. PKI is only used to encrypt the secret password itself, in this case, `Shamma_ Lamma&&Ding!$Dong`. PKI is how I tell you that the letter I'm about to send (or have sent) needs `Shamma_Lamma&&Ding!$Dong` to be decrypted without the fuzz knowing it. `Shamma_Lamma&&Ding!$Dong` is the key that actually encrypts the letter's contents. Now we need to encrypt this passcode in a way that I can exchange it with you securely, all the while knowing the fuzz is listening to our phone call just waiting for me to tell you the code. At the risk of being confusing, we have to encrypt the *key* we used to encrypt the letter. To do this, we have to use *yet another key* – this is the key used to encrypt the passcode originally used to encrypt and decrypt the letter!

To do this, you will create a key-pair: a public and a private key. This particular implementation of PKI is called "RSA," as I mentioned before. The acronym "RSA" represents the initials of the guys who came up with the paradigm. On a side note, and this is true, another guy named Clifford Cocks actually came up with it first. But the RSA guys were first to publish it. I think it was a good thing, too – going to California for the RSA Conference is one thing, but taking a buddy to the San Francisco Cocks Conference would make me feel a bit odd. Regardless, no one remembers the names of the other guys, so we just use "RSA."

Anyway, like I said, **you** create the key pair. You then tell me the *public key* over the phone. The NSA is listening, but we don't care. All the public key can do is encrypt data. It can't decrypt. If the NSA used it to *encrypt* data for some reason, you would still be the only one who could decrypt it. So first, you tell me your public key. I take that public key, and use it to encrypt the passcode

`Shamma_Lamma&&Ding!$Dong`. Once this code is encrypted with your public key, even *I* can't decrypt it. That's why no one cares about the public key – data encrypted with it can only be decrypted by *you*. To be pedantic, it can only be decrypted by the one who holds the private key associated with the public key. Now that I've encrypted `Shamma_Lamma&&Ding!$Dong` with your public key, I "read off" the encrypted password to you over the phone. The format of the data will all be binary, so when I read it to you, it will sound like Klingon. Anyway, you get the encrypted data, and use your private key to *decrypt* it. Now you know the password for the letter itself!! You know it's `Shamma_Lamma&&Ding!$Dong`. I can now send you the encrypted letter (if I haven't already) and you can decrypt it because you have the password. And that password was encrypted with a key exchanged "publicly" so that no one but us knows what it is. If the NSA duplicates the letter to keep, it will never be decrypted. Not in a billion years, or until Keith Richards dies – whichever comes first.

The Math

Let's review. In this scenario, two types of encryption are actually being used. One is *asynchronous*, and the other is *synchronous*. When I encrypted `Shamma_Lamma&&Ding!$Dong` for you, I used one particular key: your public key. When you decrypted it, you used another, *different* key: your private key. This type of encryption is called asynchronous – one key encrypts, and a different key decrypts. The encryption of the letter itself used a different manner of encryption. When I encrypted the letter with the key `Shamma_Lamma&&Ding!$Dong`, you used the same key to decrypt the data. That's called synchronous: the same key encrypts and decrypts.

Now, at this point you may be saying to yourself, "Self, why didn't they just use the one key they got the first time and encrypt the letter with that?" Well, your self has asked you a good question. When you consider how it can be that one password encrypts and another password decrypts, you might say "WTF? How could that possibly work?" Well, it's voodoo. No one knows that, but it is. OK, maybe there's a tiny bit of math too. I'll attempt to simplify the overall process in the following text.

Figuring out how to encrypt with one passcode/key and decrypt with another is a super hard thing to do. As such, the actual amount of data you can encrypt is super small. It could be bigger, but it would take ages to encrypt. To be specific, an RSA 1024-bit key (the public and private key lengths) can only encrypt a total of 116 bytes. An RSA 2048-bit key length can encrypt about 245 bytes. That would be a 245 "letter" letter. Sorry, a 245 "character" letter.

Now, you could certainly encrypt "Hey baby, whatcha wearin'?" and be done with it, but obviously we need to be able to encrypt WAY more data than that.

That's where the "symmetric" encryption comes in. You send me the public key, and before I encrypt the password to use, I chose a big random key. This will depend on the cipher, of course, but we'll use AES256. AES is the algorithm, and 256 is the key length. That's really big for a symmetric key. So, I get that really big AES number (key) and use that to encrypt the letter (this time it's not Shamma… it's the large, random key). I then use your public key to encrypt the AES key, and send it to you. You decrypt the AES key and, subsequently, as a different operation, you use the now-decrypted AES key to decrypt the letter. See, symmetric encryption, since it's pretty straightforward, can encrypt as much data as you want. It basically takes blocks of data, encrypts it, and then takes another block of data, encrypts it, and keeps going until there's no more data to encrypt. You generate the key, and it encrypts little bits at a time and sticks it all together on the other side. By the way, this is also the way your SSL connection works when you do whatever it is that you are doing that requires SSL.

Deeper Explanation

Ready for more? Of course you are! This is where the real meat, and whatever you want to go with your meat, comes in. Unless you don't eat meat, and you can just eat the "whatever it was" bits. Everyone seems to like to dance over this asymmetric magic. They all tell you, "Your public key is public! And your private key is private!" But they don't explain HOW! I mean, how can that work? How can you send me a number (key), out in front of God and everybody, which I use to encrypt, but when I send the encrypted data back, only you can decrypt it?? There's got to be some sort of relationship between the two, right? Yup.

The first concept to consider towards realizing how this can possibly work is to understand that a public key is not really "a key." A private key is not really "a key." Rather, they are both units of data comprised of several mathematical elements. I've heard many folks describe the key as, well, as a key – or better stated, a *single unit* of mathematical significance. This simple distinction may already be giving you clues on how this works. You may be thinking, "Why the hell don't they just say that?" It's for the same reason engineers call a guitar pickup a *piezoelectric transducer*, and why doctors call dust in your lungs *Pneumonoultramicroscopicsilicovolcanoconiosis*; they get more money for using big words to describe the things.

So, here's what happens. When you go to create your "keys," several processes are executed. First, we generate two very large prime numbers. We'll keep these two big prime numbers and call one p and one q. We then multiply p and q together, getting the product of the two large primes, which is a huge number. The mathematical formula for this is $pq=(p*q)$. Again, the product of the two is pq. At this point, we need to generate a number that creates a relationship to pq called a *relatively prime* number (again to be pedantic, the term "relatively prime" refers to both numbers). The two numbers are "relatively prime" when they don't share a common factor; meaning any common number where different integers could form the product. This new number is also called the *Stranger*.

On a side note, (please don't let this confuse you) the Stranger is not really a Stranger to the product pq as one may be led to believe. It is a Stranger to the product of $(p-1)*(q-1)$. You see, all prime number are odd as in ending in a 1, 3, 5 ,7, or 9. Finding a Stranger to pq could be a very long process. To help with that, we create an even number, $(p-1)*(q-1)$, and solve for *its* stranger. So, we subtract 1 from each of the two large prime numbers p and q. Two even numbers multiplied together is always an even number. This reduces the number of possible factors required to iterate through before finding a Stranger. Basically, it's faster to find the Stranger if one number is odd and the other even. Anyway, we find a Stranger to the product of $(p-1)*(q-1)$. We're going to call the Stranger d. By the way, I'm not just making up the letters. They are standard for RSA algorithms. Now, this is going to sound way more complicated than it is, but we now have to get the *multiplicative inverse* of d. This is accomplished by simply putting a 1 over it and make it a fraction as $1/d$. But now we need to get the *modulus* of $(p-1)*(q-1)$! This is easy – simply divide the multiplicative inverse by d and whatever is left over is the modulus. We call the result e.

So where are we? We've got p, q, pq, $(p-1)*(q-1)$, d, and e. With all of these variables defined, we now have everything we need to create the actual key-pairs. To create the *private* key, we'll keep p and q, which again allows us to yield the product pq. We then take d (the Stranger) and package that up with p & q. That's it – that's the private key. It is now a data unit containing p, q, and d. The *public* key, however, is only given pq – that is, the product of $p * q$, but not p and q *individually*. That's the important bit. We then package up pq with e. That's the public key. The public key only has the product pq and the multiplicative identity of the Stranger. We now have our "keys." The product pq can be given to everyone because the algorithm to decrypt the data requires p and q individually. People in the public, if snooping, would only have pq. It's like this: To make it simple, let's say I use the large prime number 5,816,267,416,546,567,109 as the basis for my public key. I put it on a bulletin board. You can do that with your public key. If someone overheard that huge key, and wanted to "crack" it, they would have to figure out which two numbers I multiplied together to get that number. You'd be at your TI-30 for a very long time factoring prime numbers one by one, as there's no other way to derive the prime components p & q from pq. But you can encrypt something for me with the huge key (and a bit of math) and when I get that encrypted data, I can decrypt it because my private key knows the two primes p & q are actually 32,416,188,271 and 179,424,779. Since I as the holder of the private key have factors of pq and the Stranger d, I can derive the key used to encrypt the data and thus decrypt it.

When you consider that all a certificate really is is a private key that you use to extract the public key in order to establish an SSL connection, it (hopefully) removes some of the "magic."

And that's why I dumped GoDaddy. Between the corporate officers shooting elephants, Marketing running sexist ads, and their initial participation with SOPA, charging me $300 for a couple of prime numbers is a bit much. And to be honest, they don't even give me the prime numbers! All they do is sign a Certificate Signing Request I create with my own privately generated key-pair!

When establishing an SSL connection, we exchange key data, encrypt an AES256 (or whatever the supported cipher is) and start talking to each other with encrypted data.

You may remember that your browser and iPhone/iPad complained about your self-signed certificate when we logged on via HTTPS and WebDAV. That's simply because the Certificate Authority (in this case, my server Grey) doesn't have its signing key stored in your browser's "default approved Certificate Authorities."

Your browser "trusts" certificates issued by this default list of people simply because they are included in the Root Certificates store of your OS. My installation of OS X came with 222 some-odd root certificates that my machine will trust, irrespective of what I may think about the companies.

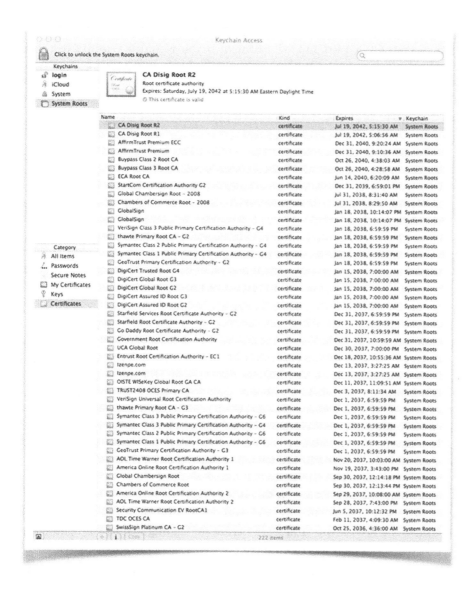

Therefore, when you go to a website using one of their certificates, your browser grabs the public key from their cert in your root store (based on its unique hash) and encrypts a message with it. The system on the other side decrypts the message, reads it, re-encrypts it with your public key, and sends it back. If the returned value matches the one you sent, you know that the system on the other side had the "real" certificate because only the service with the private key corresponding to the public key you used to encrypt the verification message could have decrypted it.

You can very well keep your self-signed certificate in order to encrypt connection to your OS X Web and Wiki content if you would like to. It's just that when people go to your site, their browser will throw up a warning about how your certificate authority could not be verified. It won't affect your encryption strength or security in the least. Further, it's trivial to simply tell your browser to "trust" that certificate and you'll never get bugged about it again.

However, this is only feasible when it comes to web clients where there is specific functionality built in that allows you to do specify trusts at will, or other client-based applications that have "custom-trust-aware" functionality.

Postfix Mail Services

In this section, we're going to set up our Postfix Mail Server service, and we're going to secure it with SSL. Therefore, we are going to need a generally trusted certificate as other SMTP servers will not establish a secure connection unless the certificate can be verified up the chain to a trusted Certificate Authority.

There are a couple of reasons to secure SMTP, though for the most part the messages you send will most probably be sent in the clear via other SMTP servers and relays that do not support encryption. Ironically, Gmail SMTP servers support SSL, which means you can connect from your SMTP server to their SMTP server over a secure channel, and send email to Gmail recipients without people in the middle being able to see what it was. I say "ironic" because Gmail reads all your email, stores keywords, and delivers customized advertising to you based on what you might have thought was a private message. That includes everyone you send to, and everyone you receive from. They also hand over that information to The Fed whenever asked for it. But I digress...

Using Certificates to Secure Services

We'll do this two ways: the easy way, and the hard(er) way. The easy way will be to use the Server App "CSR," or Certificate Signing Request, functionality to generate a CSR and send it along to the CA of our choosing.

As previously stated, I used to do business with GoDaddy, as I got what is called a "SAN" Certificate, which supports the Subject Alternate Name feature, for about $86 a year. The SAN certificate allows me to assign multiple host names to a single certificate so that one cert can be used for, say, mail.hammerofgod.com, www.hammerofgod.com, sftp.hammerofgod.com, etc. That way I can just distribute the same certificate to the various services I use where multiple hostnames are necessary.

When I went to reinstate my SAN for the purposes of this book, GoDaddy had raised their prices to $150 a year for the same, exact thing. That, I'm afraid, is ridiculous. It's a "standard" cert which doesn't require extended validation of anything else. It's the simple generation of a signed certificate which used my CSR (created with a private key only I have) to be created.

So, I told my GoDaddy rep to go jump, and bought a full-on "wildcard" SSL certificate from SSLS.com (Namecheap, Inc.). The wildcard certificate allows me to use any hostname I want with the cert. That gives me unlimited hosts supported by the same cert. For $99 I got what GoDaddy wanted $300 for. That's all it took for me to make GoDaddy GoAwayDaddy.

Before we discuss how to get a wildcard certificate installed for use with our OS X services, I'm going to show you how to create a single-host CSR (again, that means Certificate Signing Request), via the Server App, so we can at least get our, in my case "www.hammerofgod.com", host secured with SSL.

From the Server App, we're going to go to the Certificates pane and select "Get a Trusted Certificate." Hitting the "plus" sign allows us to enter the specific information we want in the certificate such as hostname, and other identifying information.

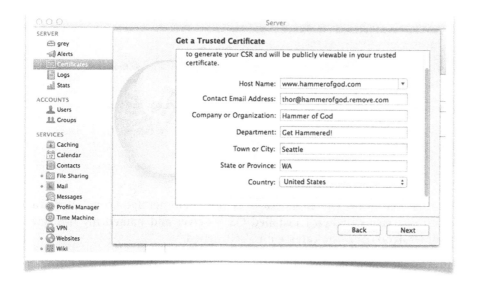

You'll notice I fudged my email address as I don't want spam automatically generated if someone wanted to go through the trouble of reading that information. In fact, when I was generating this cert, I didn't have to put in any "real" information at all. The certificate package I purchased from SSLS.com for the www.hammerofgod.com certificate was $9 for the year (compared to $50 for the exact same thing from SchmoDaddy).

This process will first create a private key which will be stored in your Keychain Access store under the hostname you entered in the CSR. Your Keychain will contain many default certificates created for use with various services (some from Apple). Here's a list of what I have:

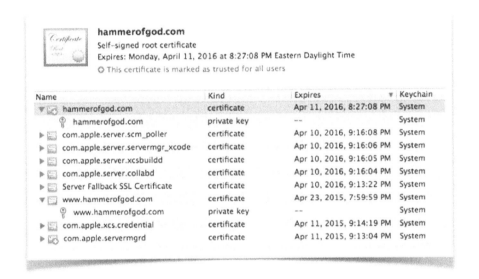

The first certificate I've highlighted is my "hammerofgod.com" certificate which was created when I installed OS X Server and named my host grey. hammerofgod.com. You can see it is "self-signed."

However, if you look down the list, you'll see an entry for "www.hammerofgod.com" (Expiring April 23, 2015) which I've expanded out to show the private key associated with that certificate.

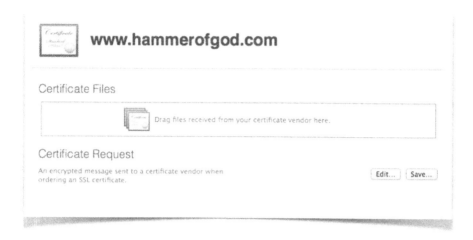

This is the key created when I asked OS X to initially generate a CSR for me. With that key, the Server App went ahead and generated the CSR using my public key. That request was encoded using Base64 and presented to me in the CSR window:

You'll probably want to save this file (defaulting to a .csr extension), but you can simply copy and paste this into the web-application your CA provides for you. When you click "Finish," the pending request will be listed in your certificates list as "pending." I then go to my CA to process the request. Here's what the SSLS.com interface looks like:

The observant of you will notice my screenshot of the pasted CSR contains different data from the screenshot of the CSR generation itself – that's just because I'm showing two different requests. You'll notice I selected "Apache + OpenSSL" as my server type because that's actually what it is.

Once this data is submitted, the CA will sign my CSR by way of creating my own certificate (.crt) file, and will zip that up for me along with the "chain" or intermediary certificate authorities required for me to have the full chain of trust accessible.

Once you get the zip file from your CA (or however you download/receive the files), you'll simply drag them from your Finder into your Server App. There's one thing you need to do first, though. When we created the private key for the host www.hammerofgod.com, we "set" the hostname and that file needs to be the same name for whatever reason. It shouldn't really matter, but that's how the Server App and its interaction with the Keychain works.

When I first received the files, my www.hammerofgod.com certificate file was named "STAR_hammerofgod_com.crt" – I simply renamed the certificate file to match www.hammerofgod.com.crt which OS X required I do.

I'm now ready to just drag those files into my "Certificate Files" box where I'll process the return certificate data and validate my www.hammerofgod.com certificate I created:

This certificate will now show up in my Server App and I can use it to secure all of my other services if I so choose. Note that I can use the host www.hammerofgod.com as my mail host all day long if I want to. It doesn't matter in the least what hostname I use in my MX (mail exchanger) DNS records. While hosts like "smtp." and "mail." are common and customary, different hostnames are only necessary when your services are published on different IP addresses.

Now we're ready to assign this cert to all the services I'll be publishing via hostname www.hammerofgod.com.

When this certificate is selected, OS X server will copy the individual chain, certificate, and key files to the /etc/certificates directly with the permissions of root:wheel (discussed in a moment).

Scripts will then be run to edit the various configuration services for Apache, Postfix, Dovecot, Messaging, etc. From a configuration standpoint, there's nothing else you have to do.

So far we've gone the "easy" route in creating our CSR, processing our certificates, and assigning those certificates to the services we want to secure.

Earlier, I discussed the fact that I purchased a "wildcard" certificate which allows me to use the cert with any hostname within my hammerofgod. com domain. By the very nature of a wildcard cert, the hostname has to be referred to with the "*" (splat/asterisk) symbol as in "*.hammerofgod.com". No problem, right? Nope, it's a problem. If you go back into Server App (at the time of this writing) and try to create a CSR using a wildcard hostname, you'll find that you can't type the * character into the interface! Doh! Server App fail!

See, even Apple does silly things sometimes, in this case resulting in a non-trivial manual hack to get around it.

However, hope is not lost. All we have to do is use the installed-by-default OpenSSL command-line utility to create our CSR. When you see how this is done, it will further demystify certificates for you. For instance, let's take this advice from TechTarget:

DEFINITION
CSR (Certificate Signing Request)

A Certificate Signing Request or CSR is a specially formatted encrypted message sent from a Secure Sockets Layer (SSL) digital certificate applicant to a certificate authority (CA). The CSR validates the information the CA requires to issue a certificate.

In a public key infrastructure (PKI) system, which enables secure data sharing among validated parties on the Internet, a CSR must be created before ordering and purchasing an SSL certificate. Applicants must first generate a key pair -- a private key which will be used to decrypt ciphertext and create digital signatures, and a public key to encrypt plaintext and verify digital certificates. Note that both the key pair and CSR must be created on the server on which the SSL certificate will be used; this is imperative to ensure the integrity of the key pair and PKI in general.

The bits you want to note are "Note that both the key pair and CSR must be created on the server on which the SSL certificate will be used; this is imperative,..."

Many times we find that free advice is worth the price! These statements are complete ca-ca as we're simply creating a private key (which includes the public key) to sign our CSR. We stuff that Base64 data into our CA's interface, and it spits out signed cert files back. That's it. You can copy these files from any server you want, to any server you want, and it will work fine. It's probably not nice to pick on these guys like that, but it bugs me when I see people giving out incorrect advice that simply muddies the technology waters. What they should have said was "if you choose to use the GUI interface for certain server products you won't be able to consume a certificate on a different server than the one the CSR was generated from."

From my iTerm bash prompt, I simply generate a new private key file along with a CSR request with this command:

```
openssl req -new -newkey rya:2048 -nodes -keyout hammerofgod.key
-out hammerofgod.csr
```

This will create my RSA 2048-bit key file, and use that to create a new CSR request. You'll see that I'm prompted to enter the relevant information which gets packaged up with my request.

The CSR text file specified is created, and you can simply copy and paste the data into the interface the same way you did before; in a few moments you'll get the zip file mailed to you.

The difference here is that since you've used OpenSSL to create the request, the referenced private key file won't be in your Keychain Access store. Bummer.

I'll show you how to handle that, but first let's see how you would manually go about doing this if you weren't using the Server App. After all, this IS the advanced chapter!

After submitting the new wildcard CSR to SSLS.com, I get the same filenames back. You'll notice that this includes the three intermediary .crt files required to validate the full trust-chain. Hold this thought.

When the Server App assigned the www.hammerofgod.com certificate to, say, my Web service, the Server App itself simply altered the Apache SSL configuration file. Specifically, it created a series of files located in my /etc/certificates folder. Here are the actual certificate files as they are copied over:

```
www.hammerofgod.com.7EC8408D0EF8A961045FB5F20F298659A5.cert.pem
www.hammerofgod.com.7EC8408D0EF8A961045FB5F20F298659A5.chain.pem
www.hammerofgod.com.7EC8408D0EF8A961045FB5F20F298659A5.concat.pem
www.hammerofgod.com.7EC8408D0EF8A961045FB5F20F298659A5.key.pem
```

These files are CHOWN'd root:wheel, which means the root user and the wheel group own the files.

After Server App copies these files, the certificates can be used to secure the services. In the case of assigning the certificate www.hammerofgod.com to

```
<IfModule mod_ssl.c>
          SSLEngine On
          SSLCertificateFile
"/etc/certificates/www.hammerofgod.com.27EC8408D0EF8A961045FB5F20F2
98659A5.cert.pem"
          SSLCertificateKeyFile
"/etc/certificates/www.hammerofgod.com.7EC8408D0EF8A961045FB5F20F29
8659A5.key.pem"
          SSLCertificateChainFile
"/etc/certificates/www.hammerofgod.com.7EC8408D0EF8A961045FB5F20F29
8659A5.chain.pem"
          SSLCipherSuite
"ALL:!aNULL:!ADH:!eNULL:!LOW:!EXP:RC4+RSA:+HIGH:+MEDIUM"
          SSLProtocol -ALL +SSLv3 +TLSv1
          SSLProxyEngine On
          SSLProxyProtocol -ALL +SSLv3 +TLSv1
     </IfModule>
```

That's all there is to it. My private key file (.key.pem) is copied, the actual certificate file (.cert.pem) is copied, and the trust chain file (.chain.pem) is copied. Those files are referenced in the respective Apache SSL configuration directives and we're good to go.

Now, you might be wondering how we got one chain file out of the three intermediate .crt files. For reference again, this is what we got:

It's simple – the chain.pem file was simply created by combining all three *AddTrustExternalCARoot.crt*, *COMODORSAAddTrustCA.crt*, and *COMODORSADomainValidationSecureServerCA.crt* files into a single file (the latter is the full name of the long filename represented with "..." snipping characters in the image). Remember, the *crt* file is nothing more than Base64 encoded certificate data and can be easily copied and pasted into a file.

In fact, that's exactly what we are going to have to do in order to make our wildcard certificate work.

I got the same files back when I submitted the new CSR for the wildcard, *.hammerofgod.com certificate. All I have to do in order to use that wildcard certificate is to put the hammerofgod.key file I created using OpenSSL during the CSR generation process in the /etc/certificates directory along with the hammerofgod.crt file sent in the .zip, and finally the three .csr files.

You can name them whatever you want, as they are only files, but I went ahead and named them the following:

    wildcard.hammerofgod.chain
    wildcard.hammerofgod.crt
    wildcard.hammerofgod.key

Again, the single .chain file was created by using a text editor to copy the contents of the three .crt files into a single file. It looks like this (with most of the lines taken out to save space):

```
-----BEGIN CERTIFICATE-----
MIIGCDCCA/CgAwIBAgIQKy5u6t1lNmwUim7bo3yMBzANBgkqhkiG9w0BAQwFADCB
hTELMAkGA1UEBhMCR0IxGzAZBgNVBAgTEkdyZWF0ZXIgTWFuY2hlc3RlcjEQMA4G
YoakRwJiNiqZ+Gb7+6kHDSVneFe0/qJakXzlByjAA6quPbYzSf
+AZxAeKCINT+b72x
-----END CERTIFICATE-----
```

```
-----BEGIN CERTIFICATE-----
MIIFdDCCBFygAwIBAgIQJ2buVutJ846r13Ci/ITeIjANBgkqhkiG9w0BAQwFADBv
MQswCQYDVQQGEwJTRTEUMBIGA1UEChMLQWRkVHJ1c3QgQUIxJjAkBgNVBAsTHUFk
XOi6wZ7I53eovNNVZ96YUWYGGjHXkBrI/V5eu+MtWuLt29G9Hvx
PUsE2JOAWVrgQSQdso8VYFhH2+9uRvOV9dlfmrPb2LjkQLPNlzmuhbsdjrzch5vR
pu/x028QOG8=
-----END CERTIFICATE-----

-----BEGIN CERTIFICATE-----
MIIENjCCAx6gAwIBAgIBATANBgkqhkiG9w0BAQUFADBvMQswCQYDVQQGEwJTRTEU
MBIGA1UEChMLQWRkVHJ1c3QgQUIxJjAkBgNVBAsTHUFkZFRydXNOIEV4dGVybmFs
IFRUUCBOZXR3b3JrMSIwIAYDVQQDExlBZGRUcnVzdCBFeHRlcm5hbCBDQSBSb290
GA1UdEwEB/wQFMAMBAf8wgZkGA1UdIwSBkTCBjoAUrb2YejSO
c4g/VhsxOBiOcQ+azcgOno4uG+GMmIPLHzHxREzGBHNJdmAPx/i9F4BrLunMTA5a
mnkPIAou1Z5jJh5VkpTYghdae9C8x49OhgQ=
-----END CERTIFICATE-----
```

When you copy these files over, they will retain the permissions they had when you downloaded them, so you'll have to CHOWN them to root:wheel by simply typing:

chown root:wheel wildcard.hammerofgod.*

That will give the files the permissions they need, and you're ready to edit your Apache SSL config file, in this case, /library/server/web/config/apache2/sites/0000_any_443_.conf file to reference the new certificate files:

```
<IfModule mod_ssl.c>
SSLEngine On
SSLCertificateFile "/etc/certificates/wildcard.hammerofgod.crt"
SSLCertificateKeyFile "/etc/certificates/wildcard.hammerofgod.key"
SSLCertificateChainFile "/etc/certificates/wildcard.hammerofgod.
chain"
SSLCipherSuite "ALL:!aNULL:!ADH:!eNULL:!LOW:!EXP:RC4+RSA:+HIGH:
+MEDIUM"
SSLProtocol -ALL +SSLv3 +TLSv1
SSLProxyEngine On
SSLProxyProtocol -ALL +SSLv3 +TLSv1
</IfModule>
```

A quick restart of the Apache service (httpd) puts us right where we want to be.

There's a consideration using this method you must be aware of. If you manually assign certificates to your services via edits in the respective .conf or .cf files, the OS X Server App certificate interface will report that you don't have any certificate assigned. That's because there won't be an associated file structure that it is expecting to match against certificates in your System hive of Keychain Access.

Not only does Server App lie to you in this regard, but as you'll see, if you choose to manually post your certificate into your Keychain Access, it will give you an even worse errant report.

I need to make sure I properly position this next bit. There certainly may be scenarios where you wish to have this particular certificate imported into your Keychain Access store. I'll show you how to do this. However, if you choose to do this with an actual wildcard certificate, binding that certificate to services via the Server App will break your services. First let's convert the certificates you received into a format where you can import them.

If you open up your Keychain Access, you can just drag the three intermediate certs into it and they will be automatically imported. However, you can't just copy over your (equivalent) of the *.hammerofgod.com cert. Why? Because it's just the signed certificate without the corresponding private key file. The CA will never have your private key – all they can do is sign your CSR and return it as a certificate file.

This is why if you DID import that cert it wouldn't show up in your Server App as an available certificate – it doesn't have a private key.

So what do we do? We just fire up OpenSSL again and tell it to create a PKCS12 certificate file – this way we can create a single PKCS certificate that contains both the cert and the private key. With the files we've already created, we'll just use this command:

```
sudo openssl pkcs12 -export -clcerts -inkey wildcard.hammerofgod.
key -in wildcard.hammerofgod.crt -out hammerofgod.p12
```

The "sudo" command will give you root privileges for this particular command. You'll have to enter your admin password to do this. Next though you'll be asked for another password, the "Export Password." This is required – if you leave it blank it will create it, but you can't import it into Keychain. Enter a decent password for your Export Password, confirm, and you'll have your PKCS12 certificate created.

You can then simply import that file into Keychain, and when you do, Server App will be more than happy to let you use it via the GUI:

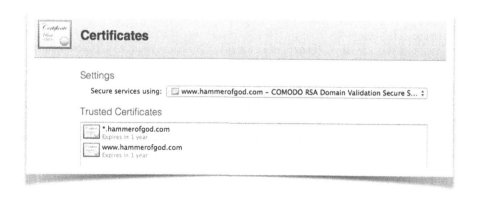

Now I'll show you the two "lies" Server App will tell you. The results illustrated in this screen shot come from two different operations. As previously mentioned, if I manually edit my Apache and Dovecot (IMAP) service configuration files to point to the wildcard.hammerofgod files, the Certificate dialog will say "None" are assigned in the GUI:

That's bad enough, but what (in my opinion) is worse is the reference to the "*.hammerofgod" certificates bound to the other services. While Server App may indeed *think* these certificates are bound to the services, and indeed they are insofar as the scripts altering the config files are concerned, it *won't work*.

Here's why. Let's examine our Postfix "main.cf" file located in the /Library/Server/Mail/Config/postfix/ directory. Here are the three configuration lines we're concerned with:

```
smtpd_tls_cert_file = /etc/certificates/*.hammerofgod.com.[some
random hash].cert.pem
smtpd_tls_key_file =
smtpd_tls_CAfile = /etc/certificates/*.hammerofgod.com.[same random
hash].chain.pem
```

The Server App thought it was doing the "right thing" here by allowing you to select the "*.hammerofgod" certificate. But what Server App scripting does is take the hostname of the certificate and create associated files in the /etc/certificates directory *using the hostname* as part of the file. You'll notice a hash is added to the filename to ensure uniqueness when it creates these files.

If not obvious, the "*" character is not only the wildcard symbol for the certificate hosts, but it is also a wildcard character as far as the *operating system* is concerned. The "splat" references all files in the OS as it does all hosts in the certificate. As such, our services will error out when that filename is parsed by the service. You'll also notice that Server App scripting was unable to figure out the actual .key file necessary so it just left the directive blank. Nice.

This manifests itself by my Postfix SMTP service breaking. To fix it, all we have to do is manually change these file references back to the "wildcard.hammerofgod" files we copied over to our /etc/certificates directory and restart the services.

The takeaway from this is for you to be very careful when using wildcard certificates. If you choose to do so (or I guess "need to" is more appropriate), then understand that you'll have to manually configure the configuration files and not use Server App to assign certificates.

This really only scratches the surface of what you can do with OS X Server, but anything more on the subject will take us a bit "out of scope" for this book. The good news is that you'll now have everything you need to support rich, reliable, and high-performance server services for you and anyone else you choose to provide them for.

Index

Note: Page numbers followed by "*f*" and "*t*" refer to figures and tables, respectively.

A

Add Network Wizard, 43
"Add Networking" function, 44
Advanced Encryption Standard
    (AES), 104
Advanced level tech, 180–181. *See
    also* Medium level tech
    Postfix Mail Services, 192–205
    starting and configuration of mail,
        181–192
Advanced media control, 67–74
AES. *See* Advanced Encryption
    Standard (AES)
Airplay, 67
    Apple TV, 71–72, 74
    Extend Desktop, 73
    functionality, 67, 69
    HDTV, 68
    Home Sharing, 67
    Man Cave, 69
    Match Desktop Size, 72
    Meadow TV, 69
    Mirroring, 70
    OS X, and iOS, 68–69
Anonymous users, 175
Apache service, 202
Apple defaults, 93–99
Apple Remote Desktop (ARD),
    124–125, 127–137
Apple TV, 71–72, 74
ARD. *See* Apple Remote Desktop
    (ARD)
Asynchronous encryption, 187
Audio Distribution Center, 57

B

BitLocker, 100

C

"Caller ID spoofing" service, 21
Certificate Signing Request (CSR),
    192, 198–199, 198*f*
chain.pem file, 201
"Choose User Profile" dialog box,
    17
CHOWN'd root:wheel, 200
ClamAV, 182
"Cloud, The", 123
Conversation, 184–187
CSR. *See* Certificate Signing Request
    (CSR)
Customization, 75–78

D

Demilitarized zone (DMZ), 31–32

E

EFS. *See* Encrypted file system (EFS)
Encrypted disk images, 99–108
Encrypted file system (EFS), 100
End User License Agreement (EULA),
    2
ESXi servers, 33
EULA. *See* End User License
    Agreement (EULA)
Exit Relay, 22–23
exit Tor, 53
Extend Desktop, 73

F

Facebook, 5
File Sharing, 126
Finder, 78–85

Firefox "profiles", 15
    "allow only" process, 18–19
    browser settings, 15–16
    "Choose User Profile" dialog box,
        17
    cookie, 18
    "Create Profile" button, 16
    functionality, 19
    "professional" or "limited"
        configuration, 19
    session in Terminal/iTerm, 16
Firefox-bin, 12–13, 12*f*
Flat network, 36

G

Greylisting, 182

H

HDTV, 68
Home Sharing, 58–59, 67
Hyper-V, 38
    virtualization servers,
        123–124

I

iCloud, 124, 168
    Back to My Mac, 137–148
IDS. *See* Intrusion Detection Systems
    (IDS)
IIS. *See* Internet Information Server
    (IIS)
Intelligent, multi-choice dialog
    boxes, 108–109
Intelligent file copy, 116–121
Intelligent shared file system updates,
    110–116

Interface
    apple defaults, 93–99
    customization, 75–78
    encrypted disk images, 99–108
    finder, 78–85
    intelligent, multi-choice dialog
        boxes, 108–109
    intelligent file copy, 116 121
    intelligent shared file system
        updates, 110–116
    multiple monitors, 75–78
    navigation, 78–85
    quick look, 85–86
    script editor, 93–99
    tagging with spotlight, 88–93
    tags, 86–88
Internet advertising, 1–2
Internet Information Server (IIS),
    165
Intrusion Detection Systems (IDS),
    41–42
iTunes, basic media sharing via, 58
    cripple-ware, 59
    Home Sharing, 59
    iPad, 62, 66
    libraries, 64
    Macs or PCs, 60
    media application, 61
    "media-type-by-media-type"
        access, 67
    music application, 63
    playlists, 59–60

J
"Junk mail" filtering, 182–183

K
"keyspace", 184–185

L
"Launch Application" applet, 126
Little Snitch, 8–10
Logical privacy and security, 1, 5.
        See also Technical privacy and
        security
    chase online banking and transfer,
        7
    damage prevention, 8
    EULA, 2
    Facebook, 5
    Google's own privacy statement,
        2–3
    internet, 5
    internet advertising, 1–2

online safety, 1
    OS X, 1
    "personal profile" information, 2
    production and internet account, 7
    recurring payment, 7
    stereo systems, 4
    transactions, 8
    WLID, 4
Low level Firefox profile and
        configuration editing, 26
    cookie table, 30–31
    cookie value, 31
    cookies database structure, 30
    OS X applications, 26
    Scratch profile, 26–27
    SQLite, 28
    SQLite Manager, 28, 29f

M
Mail, 181–192. See also Postfix Mail
        Services
    conversation, 184–187
    deeper explanation, 188–192
    Math, 187–188
    PKI, 184
Man Cave, 57, 69
Match Desktop Size, 72
Math, 187–188
MeadowTV, 58, 69
Media Center Extenders, 55
"Media-type-by-media-type" access,
    67
Medium level tech, 161–180. See also
        Advanced level tech
Microsoft, 159–160
Microsoft Azure Cloud Services, 123
Microsoft solution (SMS), 137
Mirroring, 70
Multiple monitors, 75–78

N
Navigation, 78–85
"Network Usage" function, 136–137

O
Objective Development, 9
Online safety, 1
OS X Server, 1, 55, 159–160, 161f
    advanced level tech, 180–181
        Postfix Mail Services, 192–205
        starting and configuration of
            mail, 181–192
    advanced media control, 67
        airplay, 67–74

"Advanced Media Streaming"
        configuration, 55
    Apple TV, 56
    Audio Distribution Center, 57
    iTunes, basic media sharing via, 58
        cripple-ware, 59
        Home Sharing, 59
        iPad, 62, 66
        libraries, 64
        Macs or PCs, 60
        media application, 61
        "media-type-by-media-type"
            access, 67
        Music application, 63
        Playlists, 59–60
    Man Cave, 57
    MeadowTV, 58
    Media Center Extenders, 55
    Media-sharing environment, 56
    medium level tech, 161–180
    objects, 57
    remotely controlling media
        services, 55
OSXodus, 166

P
PKI. See Public key infrastructure (PKI)
Port forwarding, 35
Postfix Mail Services, 192–205. See
        also Mail
    using certificates to secure services,
        192–205
    CSR, 198–199, 198f
Postfix SMTP service breaking, 205
Private Cloud, 34
Private key, 188–190
Public key, 188–191
Public key infrastructure (PKI), 104,
    184, 186

Q
Quick look, 85–86

R
Relatively prime number, 188–189
relaunch Tor, 53
Remote Access, 123
    ARD, 127–137
    iCloud's Back to My Mac, 137–148
    SSH supplement, 148–158
    VNC, 124–127
Remote Desktop, 153
Remote Logon, 148
Remote Management, 127

Rivest-Shamir-Adelman algorithm
    (RSA algorithm), 104
Routing modem, 35
RSA algorithm. *See* Rivest-Shamir-
    Adelman algorithm (RSA
    algorithm)

S

SBS. *See* Small Business Server (SBS)
SCP. *See* Secure copy (SCP)
"Screen Sharing" application, 126,
    146–147
Script editor, 93–99
Search engines, 20–21
Secure copy (SCP), 152
Secure Shell (SSH), 148–158
Small Business Server (SBS),
    159–160
SMS. *See* Microsoft solution (SMS)
SMTP, 181–182, 192
Sockets Secure protocol (SOCKS
    protocol), 54
SOCKS protocol. *See* Sockets Secure
    protocol (SOCKS protocol)
SocksPort, 51–52
Spotlight, tagging with, 88–93
SQL. *See* Structured Query Language
    (SQL)
SQLite, 28
SSH. *See* Secure Shell (SSH)
Stereo systems, 4
Structured Query Language (SQL), 28
Symmetric encryption, 188
Synchronous encryption, 187
System Registry, 26

T

Tags, 86–88
Target Disk Mode, 120

Technical privacy and security, 8–9.
    See also Logical privacy and
    security
    alternate search engines, 20–21
    cookies, 10–11
    default installation of Firefox, 11
    Firefox "profiles", 15–19
    Firefox-bin, 12–13, 12f
    Little Snitch's capability, 9–12
    low level Firefox profile and
        configuration editing, 26–31
    normal browsing scenarios, 10
    Objective Development, 9
    TOR proxy, 21–25
    virtual DMZ environment, shared
        Tor proxy in, 31–54
TOR proxy, 21–22, 23f
    "caller ID spoofing" service, 21
    Exit Relay, 22–23
    IP, 21
    "No Proxy Detected", 24
    OS X Tor application, 22
    relay-to-relay connection process,
        24
    sending automated queries, 25

U

UNIX command, 132

V

virtual DMZ environment, shared Tor
    proxy in, 31
    Bridge Relay, 32–33
    client-by-client basis, 31–32
    ESXi, 33, 39
        Add Network Wizard, 43
        "Add Networking" function, 44
        datacenter, 35
        ESX.1, 37

exit Tor and relaunch Tor, 53
flat network, 36, 41
Hyper-V, 38
IDS, 41–42
LAN IP addresses, 35
"observed IP ranges", 40
OS X installation, 50
physical NICs, 37
port forwarding, 35
Private Cloud, 34
routing modem, 35
SOCKS protocol, 54
SocksPort, 51–52
SSH and SCP, 49–50
vCenter product, 33–34
Virtual Machine Port Group, 38
"vKernel" port group, 39, 45, 47
"VM Network1.1" port group,
    40
vSwitch, 38–39
functionality, 32
Virtual Machine Port Group, 38
Virtual Network Computing (VNC),
    124–127
Virtual Private Network (VPN), 124
Virtual switch (vSwitch), 37
"vKernel" port group, 37, 39
VMWare virtualization service, 124
VNC. *See* Virtual Network
    Computing (VNC)
VPN. *See* Virtual Private Network
    (VPN)
vSwitch. *See* Virtual switch (vSwitch)

W

Web Distributed Authoring and
    Versioning (WebDAV), 176
Wiki Document Management, 168
Windows Live ID (WLID), 4

Printed in the United States
By Bookmasters